Cultivating Critical Advocacy

A Framework for Educators of Multilingual Learners

Rebecca E. Linares and Kate Seltzer

NEW YORK AND LONDON

Designed cover image: Getty Images

First published 2027
by Routledge
605 Third Avenue, New York, NY 10158

and by Routledge
4 Park Square, Milton Park, Abingdon, Oxon, OX14 4RN

Routledge is an imprint of the Taylor & Francis Group, an informa business

ISBN: 978-1-041-04552-6 (pbk)
ISBN: 978-1-003-62877-4 (ebk)

DOI: 10.4324/9781003628774

Typeset in Palatino
by Apex CoVantage, LLC

Cultivating Critical Advocacy

As the number of students designated as Multilingual Learners (MLs) continues to grow, educators must think critically about how best to support them. This hands-on guide introduces *critical advocacy* and explores how its effectiveness is tied to educators' critical awareness of themselves, their broader political contexts, and their daily school-based work with MLs.

The authors use a tree metaphor to represent the importance of roots (identities, beliefs, and ideologies); the trunk (core critical advocacy beliefs); branches (areas of critical advocacy action); and off-shoots and leaves (local critical advocacy action). Throughout, there are features such as *Voices From the Field* and *Digging In,* which invite readers to consider concepts from the text in their own lives, contexts, and practices. At the end of the book, the authors provide a Critical Advocacy Action Planning Tool to help readers plan for critical advocacy in their own context.

Whether you already see yourself as an advocate or are new to this work, this book will help you develop a critical advocacy stance and cultivate the practices and dispositions needed to engage in meaningful, sustainable, and effective advocacy with and for MLs in your school, classroom, and community.

Rebecca E. Linares began working with multilingual students and families through after-school programming for refugee and immigrant K-8 students in Kentucky. Her research examines the transnational literacy and translanguaging practices of emergent multilingual adolescents. She is an associate professor in the ESL/Bilingual Education program at Rowan University in New Jersey.

Kate Seltzer got her start in education as a high school English Language Arts teacher in New York City. She is co-author of the book *The Translanguaging Classroom: Leveraging Student Bilingualism for Learning,* and her research overall focuses on critical, asset-oriented approaches to educating MLs. She is an associate professor in the ESL/Bilingual Education program at Rowan University in New Jersey.

Equity and Social Justice in Education Series

Paul C. Gorski, Series Editor

Routledge's Equity and Social Justice in Education series is a publishing home for books that apply critical and transformative equity and social justice theories to the work of on-the-ground educators. Books in the series describe meaningful solutions to the racism, white supremacy, economic injustice, sexism, heterosexism, transphobia, ableism, neoliberalism, and other oppressive conditions that pervade schools and school districts.

Navigating Power, Harnessing Possibility: A Guide for Leading Schools Through Uncertain Times
Mary Rice-Boothe

Community, Love, and Connection in Early Care and Education: An Interactive Guide for Holistic, Equitable Early Learning
Meghan L. Green, Lilly Padia, and Mariana Souto-Manning

Transformative Mindfulness in Education: Caring for Ourselves While Kindling Change
Rhiannon Kim

Teaching Indigenous Studies: An Introduction for K-12 Educators
Leilani Sabzalian, Meredith McCoy, and Helen Thomas

Peacebuilding Pedagogies: Racial Justice, Dialogue, and Belonging in the Classroom
Crystena Parker-Shandal

Cultivating Critical Advocacy: A Framework for Educators of Multilingual Learners
Rebecca E. Linares and Kate Seltzer

Contents

Preface

As researchers and scholars in the field of bilingual education, we have regularly witnessed and been inspired by the powerful ways educators engage in meaningful, sustainable, and effective advocacy with and on behalf of multilingual learners. At the same time, as teacher educators, we find ourselves regularly asking what it looks like to support teachers in developing an understanding of advocacy as an ongoing, constantly evolving practice and way of being.

After wrestling with these questions semester after semester and engaging pre- and in-service teachers in various activities designed to support the development of an advocacy stance, we realized that a larger, *critical, action-oriented* approach was necessary, one that accounted for the reality that to be an advocate with and for others, we must begin by looking *critically* at our own identities, ideologies, and beliefs. From here, we began developing the critical advocacy framework presented in this book.

This framework is based on our own experiences and those of educators around the country who identify as critical advocates. Their words and commitments, which you'll find throughout this book, solidified our belief that those who identify as advocates must critically examine themselves, their broader political contexts, and their daily school-based work with MLs before, during, and after engaging in advocacy action.

Our hope is that this book and the critical advocacy framework will serve as a tool, resource, and source of support for educators at all stages of their careers and critical advocacy journeys.

Acknowledgments

To the critical advocates we spoke to and to the countless others who do this work every day: your passion, dedication, and commitment to multilingual learners give us so much hope, even in dark times.

To our families: you are the roots of our own critical advocacy, and we continue to grow because you nourish us.

Introduction

Advocacy Is . . .

> [Recognizing that] now that I'm a citizen, I'm able to advocate for those that can't, just like there were DREAMers that, when I was a kid, were advocating for . . . me even though they didn't know me; they were advocating for people like me. Now it's my turn to step up; it's my turn to advocate for those that have to hide right now.
>
> – Martha, Spanish-English Dual Language teacher, Kentucky

> Learning as much as I can about my students, their families, and their backgrounds.
>
> – Katie, English Language Development teacher, Colorado

> Passionately ensuring [MLs] get access to the curriculum rather than . . . doing alternative activities during class.
>
> – Tammy, former English Learner teacher and current elementary school Vice Principal, California

DOI: 10.4324/9781003628774-1

What Is Critical Advocacy?

We open this book with the words of educators from across the US who consider themselves advocates of multilingual learners (MLs).[1] As they illustrate, being an advocate involves direct action as well as reflection, dialogue, and engagement. In that spirit, this book isn't as much about the *what*, meaning the topics and issues faced by MLs across US schools that require advocacy efforts. This book is more about the *how*, meaning how teachers and other educators across different contexts can participate in what we call *critical advocacy* for MLs.

So what is critical advocacy? As the three previously mentioned advocates demonstrate, we believe that school-based advocacy for MLs – efforts that seek to improve MLs' educational experiences – must be rooted in hope, empathy, and a drive to ensure equity and access. It requires a *critical* focus on actions that are meaningful, sustainable, and effective for MLs and for advocates themselves. We believe that such actions can only be accomplished when advocates gain critical awareness of themselves, their broader political contexts, and their daily school-based work with MLs. Such critical awareness is gained through honest reflection on what Kate (Seltzer, 2022) has called the personal, the political, and the pedagogical.

Examining the *personal* means exploring how our own backgrounds and histories shape our approaches to working with MLs. This criticality goes beyond calls to "check our privilege" or simply recognize our own biases. Critical self-reflection helps us better understand and locate ourselves so that we can participate in advocacy efforts more ethically. For advocates like Martha, it means recognizing how her status as a formerly undocumented child in the U.S. shapes her desire to engage in self-advocacy and advocacy for others. She recognizes the privileges that were not afforded to her and now leverages them in her advocacy for MLs.

Thinking critically about the *political* means acknowledging the inherently political nature of all school-based decision-making related to MLs. Critical advocacy recognizes that the challenges MLs face in schools are inextricably linked to powerful social forces (i.e., racism, xenophobia) that shape systems and contribute to structural inequalities. For educators like Katie, learning about her students, their families, and their communities, as well as what their strengths and needs are, not only develops her empathy and compassion but also allows her to understand how larger social forces manifest and affect MLs at the individual level.

Lastly, a focus on the *pedagogical* means understanding that our school-based work with MLs – from teaching to coaching to parent/family coordination to leadership – is *also* political. As advocates like Tammy illustrate, being critical of the pedagogical means ensuring MLs have access to rigorous, standards-aligned instruction that supports their learning and dignifies them as intelligent, capable people. The pedagogical decisions we make about programming (e.g., students' placement in bilingual vs. English-medium classrooms), the curricula we adopt, and the languages we use in our classrooms and schools have the potential to disrupt inequitable schooling experiences of MLs.

Why Critical Advocacy *Right Now*?

As Martha's definition of advocacy reminds us, this is not the first nor the last time that MLs, their families, and their communities have been under attack. We began writing this book in early 2025, as the political, linguistic, and educational landscape was becoming more and more precarious for MLs and those who educate them. Depending on our own personal identities, political stances, and pedagogical practices, this precarity made many of us want to turn inward, to protect ourselves and our own families and circles. At the same time, it served as a call to action: a reminder that our work advocating with and for marginalized populations is ongoing, and that we must shift in response to the constraints and realities of the moment. In this book, we invite you – educators who work with MLs – to gain deeper understandings of who you are, the broader political contexts in which you work, and your daily school-based work with MLs. It is our hope that this exploration helps you to uncover and further develop what it means to be a critical advocate in your local contexts. This book comes at a time when many of us may feel galvanized to take action, seeking community and solidarity as we work to challenge the harsh and inequitable realities of the moment. We ourselves feel this call to action and invite you to join us in exploring what it means to "show up" with and for MLs, their families, and their communities.

Critical advocacy is not just about meeting the needs of the current moment; it is about imagining and working toward more hopeful futures for MLs and for ourselves as advocates. As we illustrate throughout the book, by engaging in critical advocacy with and for MLs, we are also fighting burnout and isolation. We are joining the efforts of a larger movement and network of advocates around the country who choose to take a stand and work toward positive change in their communities. As Ernest Morrell (2015), the renowned literacy scholar and one of Kate's mentors who passed away only months before this book's publication, reminds us,

> Nobody has time for us to twiddle our thumbs and be hopeless . . . what [people] are counting on is that we are nurturing hope. So if we don't like the way things are, we have to change them.
>
> (p. 322)

In writing this book, we refuse hopelessness. We hope this book reminds you, as it has reminded us, that there is important personal, political, and pedagogical work to do. That work is far from easy, but it is integral to building more just futures for MLs.

The Critical Advocacy Tree

To help us further explain the integrated nature of the personal, political, and pedagogical aspects of critical advocacy, we present the metaphor of a tree. In conceptualizing this metaphor, we drew inspiration from Hammond's (2014) analogy of *culture* as a tree. Like Hammond, we believe it is essential that we consider the larger ecosystems in which critical advocacy takes place and recognize that growth happens in response to the seasons and environments in which we are planted. Our whole book is organized around this tree, and includes what we describe as the roots, trunk, branches, and off-shoots and leaves of critical advocacy (Figure 0.1).

The Roots: Our Identities, Beliefs, and Ideologies

The roots represent the foundation of critical advocacy. They symbolize how our advocacy efforts are grounded in our own

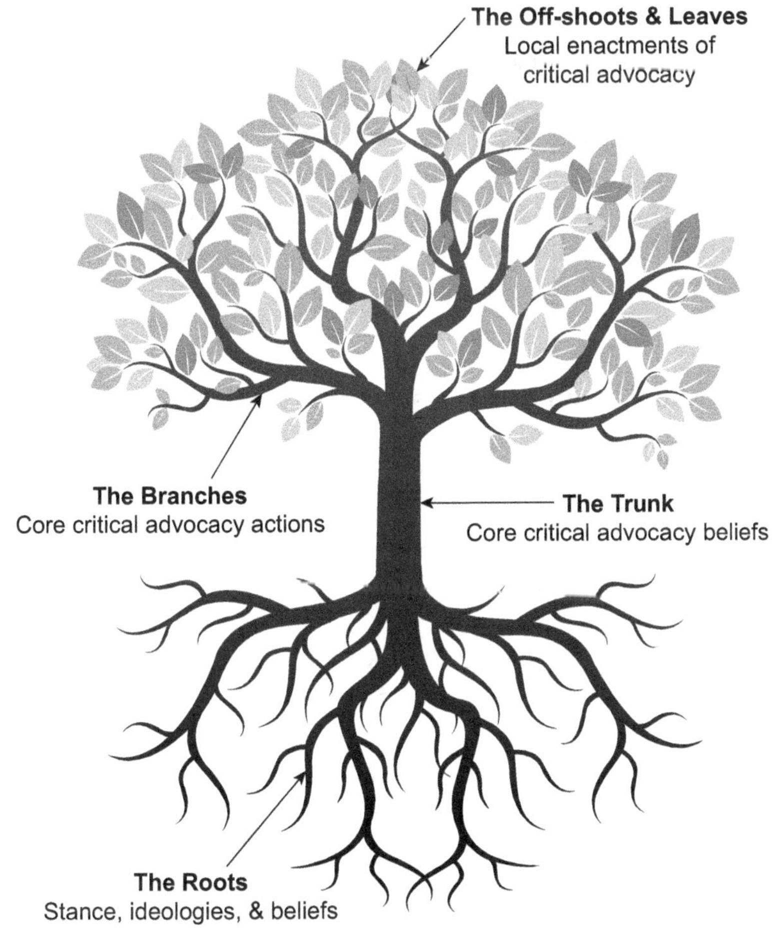

FIGURE 0.1 THE CRITICAL ADVOCACY TREE.

histories and ongoing life experiences. Critical advocates constantly reflect on how they are *already* rooted and how they might *extend* those root systems outward, beyond their existing knowledge and experiences. In Chapter 1, we share our stories and delve into important elements of our own roots: our linguistic, cultural, and racial identities, our backgrounds and lived experiences, and the elements of our personal and professional lives that have drawn us to critical advocacy. And because we believe that our roots grow and are influenced by larger forces and ideologies that permeate our soil, Chapter 2 invites you to interrogate your own beliefs about advocacy and to begin exploring how those beliefs shape your work with MLs.

The Trunk: Core Critical Advocacy Beliefs

The trunk of the tree represents the core critical advocacy beliefs that are shaped and nourished by our roots and that simultaneously shape and nourish the rest of the tree. Though all critical advocates will have their own unique core beliefs, we see the following three, which we explore in depth in Chapter 3, as integral to critical advocacy and to the strength and steadiness of our efforts:

1. Empathy and compassion are central to advocacy work with MLs;
2. Collaboration and community-building strengthen advocacy work; and
3. Perpetual learning is key to evolving our beliefs, practices, and advocacy efforts.

In our conversations and work with educators of MLs across the country, we have found that empathy and compassion are central to their professional *and* personal lives. We've also seen how a belief in the power of collaboration and community can shift advocates away from visions of individual "heroes" toward building connections with like-minded people and members of the communities they serve. Lastly, a commitment to perpetual learning ensures that critical advocacy is not seen as a destination but as a dynamic process that enables us to grow and evolve.

The Branches: Core Areas of Critical Advocacy Action

The branches that grow from a strong trunk represent what we define as core areas of critical advocacy action. By this, we mean that although local context shapes advocacy, there are some areas that will *always* be important when advocating for/with MLs:

1. Pedagogical decision-making;
2. Relationship-building and community connections;
3. Local policy-making; and
4. Disrupting deficit ideologies of MLs.

These branches, which we discuss alongside the off-shoots and leaves (i.e., local advocacy actions) that sprout from them in Chapter 4, represent how critical advocacy beliefs are enacted in school communities.

The Off-Shoots and Leaves: Local Critical Advocacy Actions

Finally, from the tree's branches grow off-shoots and leaves. These represent the many small, locally specific critical advocacy actions that bloom and sprout for different purposes, audiences, times, and goals. In addition to featuring examples of these local critical advocacy efforts in Chapter 4, we also draw on them to illustrate that advocacy work rarely, if ever, occurs without challenges. Chapter 5 explores these challenges, focusing on how critical advocates can, as the organizer Mariame Kaba (2025) puts it, fortify themselves for the ongoing struggle. In Chapter 6, we provide four in-depth scenarios that require critical advocates to grow their own off-shoots and leaves in ways that both account for potential challenges and result in meaningful, sustainable, and effective advocacy for MLs.

Ultimately, we have written this book for anyone who wants to develop and evolve their critical advocacy for MLs. To that end, Chapter 7 presents a framework for Critical Advocacy Action Planning, which invites you to identify an issue that is important to you and the MLs you work with and create a thoughtful plan that will help you enact critical advocacy in your own context. Though we include the Critical Advocacy Action Planning Tool at the end of the book, each chapter will prompt you to connect what you read to this planning. We hope this resource serves as a culmination of the knowledge and insights you have gained while working through this book.

Features of This Book

We recognize that readers come to this book from many different perspectives and levels of experience with advocacy. Some of you may be at the beginning of your advocacy journey, while others may consider yourselves seasoned and experienced, but in need of new approaches and inspiration. For this reason, we have integrated the following features throughout the book:

Voices From the Field

In preparation for writing this book, we spoke with educators across the US who identify as advocates for MLs. These individuals work as general education, ESL, and bilingual classroom teachers, ML program coordinators and directors, family engagement, language development, and evaluation specialists, instructional coaches, and more. We began this introductory chapter with their voices, and we will feature their words and stories throughout the book to bring critical advocacy to life and to illustrate how individuals engage in advocacy for MLs across a variety of settings and circumstances.

Digging In

In this recurring feature, we invite you to consider concepts from the text in your own life, context, and practice. These include questions that invite your critical thinking, resources for further learning, and relevant literature and research that connect to our ideas.

 Critical Advocacy Action Planning Connection

In Chapter 7, you will be invited to think about a question or issue you face in your context that lends itself to critical advocacy for MLs. Though that planning is very action-oriented, one of our key messages in this book is that it is not *only* our actions that matter, but the thinking and reflection that occur before, during, and after our actions. This feature will help you make connections between the content of each chapter and the kind of thinking you can bring to your critical advocacy action planning.

Conclusion

In keeping with our belief in the power of collaboration and community, we encourage you to read this book with others – on your own time, in professional learning communities, book clubs, or other professional development settings. We know that advocacy can feel lonely, so it is powerful to cultivate a group of people who share commitments and seek to put their beliefs into practice. We hope this book will bring you together with like-minded colleagues, community members, ML students, and others who are what Love (2019) calls co-conspirators to develop your critical advocacy. May this book serve as a guide and source of support as you work to make the experiences and outcomes for MLs in your community more equitable. Let's get our hands in the dirt and begin.

Digging In: Defining Your Advocacy

Like the educators we quoted at the beginning of this introduction, each of us has our own definition of advocacy. To start your own critical advocacy journey, we invite you – and ideally the others you're reading this book alongside – to define advocacy through four words. You can see how advocate and educator Valentina Gonzalez did in Figure 0.2:

FIGURE 0.2 "HOW TO BE A CHANGE MAKER" INFOGRAPHIC.

Reprinted with permission.

1. Think of four words or short phrases that help you define advocacy.
2. Explain, draw, or otherwise represent those four words.
3. Share your words and ideas with others, discussing any similarities or differences in your definitions.

Note

1 We refer to this population of students as multilingual learners (MLs) to challenge the deficit-oriented nature inherent in the label "English Learner" adopted in the Every Student Succeeds Act (2015), as it legitimizes learners' entire linguistic repertoire rather than solely privileging English. We recognize that different states utilize different terms, so we have maintained those terms when describing job titles of the critical advocates we feature in the book.

Part I

Establishing Roots and Strengthening the Trunk of Critical Advocacy

Part I of this book delves into the foundational features of the critical advocacy tree: its roots and trunk. Understanding our roots means understanding how the terrain of our upbringing and early experiences has shaped their growth as well as how those roots have continued to grow and expand over time. Understanding our trunk means understanding how your roots have nourished and strengthened the beliefs that make up the core of your work with multilingual learners (MLs).

We all have roots that anchor us and support our growth. "Roots" traditionally symbolize where we come from – the cultural, familial, or even regional roots that shape who we are and how we move through the world. We understand the power of the roots that are forged in our youth and through the formative years of our lives. Those roots shape us and help us forge the core beliefs that make our advocacy steady and strong. However, we also focus on the perpetual and expansive rooting that occurs as we respond to our changing contexts and understandings, which makes our critical advocacy dynamic and ever-evolving.

In Chapter 1, we delve into this dual understanding of roots, which lays out who we, Rebecca and Kate, are and how we have established and expanded our own roots. This chapter also invites you to explore your own roots, including how they are shaped by complex, intersecting elements of your identity, how they have responded to the contexts in which they grow, and how they have expanded through alternative experiences and counter-narratives.

If our roots and trunk are shaped by the contexts in which they grow, we must acknowledge the deficit-oriented ideologies that permeate discourse around MLs. Chapter 2 describes problematic framings of advocacy that are often unintentionally informed and shaped by these ideologies and discusses how

DOI: 10.4324/9781003628774-2

critical advocates can strengthen the trunk of their tree with asset-oriented, empowering understandings of MLs. Chapter 3 puts forth three core beliefs informed by these asset-oriented understandings that make up the strong trunk of the critical advocacy tree. These beliefs help advocates ensure that their efforts are meaningful, sustainable, and effective by centering empathy, collaboration, and perpetual learning.

This first part of the book may challenge you, in that it asks you to interrogate parts of yourself and your ideologies you may not have known you had. The ideas and opportunities to dig in that we offer in these first three chapters are meant to support you on this journey, never to mire you in feelings of shame. We hope you'll agree that the challenge is worth it, and that this first part of our book helps strengthen your beliefs and emboldens you to take critical advocacy action for MLs.

1

The Roots of Critical Advocacy

Our own backgrounds and histories inherently shape what we do. For this reason, delving into the personal – the roots of our tree – is an essential first step for developing critical advocacy. We begin by sharing narratives of our own backgrounds and histories, both to introduce ourselves and to draw attention to how our roots – and the process of identifying, naming, and unpacking what has shaped them – inform our work. We then highlight three central points about roots and the role they play in critical advocacy. First, we assert that our roots are shaped by the complex, intersecting elements of our identities. Second, we believe our roots respond to the contexts in which they grow, including dominant beliefs and ideologies. And last, we contend that our roots expand through alternative experiences and counter-narratives. Overall, this chapter invites you to look closely at your own roots, digging deeper into who you are and how you locate yourself in your work with multilingual learners (MLs).

Our Roots: Rebecca's and Kate's Stories

Rebecca's Story

I grew up in a Peruvian and Cuban Spanish-dominant home in a predominantly white monolingual community in Kentucky, where I attended an English-medium K-8 Catholic school and

DOI: 10.4324/9781003628774-3

public magnet high school. My father is an immigrant from Peru, and my mother is a first-generation New Yorker who spent much of her adolescence in Spain after her family left Cuba in the early 1960s. Outside of close friends, I do not recall discussing my family's cultural or linguistic background. And while Spanish was a language I was immersed in at home, it was not until seventh grade that I gained access to formal Spanish language instruction. In their excitement that my siblings and I would now have access to Spanish at school, my parents offered to outfit the Spanish classroom with Latin American art and decorations, primarily from Peru, Cuba, and Mexico, where my aunt lived. Seeing decorations and cultural artifacts in the classroom that had originally been displayed in our home felt awkward. Out of embarrassment and fear of distinguishing myself from my peers, I did not share that my parents had lent the materials to the school. In fact, the only time my parents' multilingualism came up at school was when a classmate remarked on my father's accented English when he chaperoned a field trip.

Though my cultural background was literally on display at school, it was not something I claimed. Instead, I struggled to reconcile this "public" recognition of our cultural and linguistic heritage with my parents' decision to speak to my brothers and me mostly in English despite their preference for and use of Spanish in their own relationship and daily lives. For much of my young adult life, I resented my parents for not explicitly cultivating my bilingualism and biliteracy and my Latina identity. My own claim of such an identity did not occur until my adolescence, when I traveled to Peru and met my extended family for the first time. Feeling like I had missed an opportunity to cultivate my identity made me resentful of my parents. Though later in life, after learning about language ideologies in graduate school, I realized that my parents likely did their best by encouraging me to build connections with my identity and family abroad while also negotiating the social pressures that they felt for us to speak English in Kentucky.

In my experience working with refugee and immigrant youth in an afterschool program in Kentucky, I witnessed firsthand the pressure adolescents felt to shed their home culture and language in exchange for English to better integrate themselves into school systems that failed to offer culturally and linguistically responsive learning opportunities. For many who found themselves in community environments and learning spaces that centered English monolingualism, there was a sense that to be seen as truly proficient in English, they had to let go of their home language.

In many ways, my participation in programs that emphasized academic support in and for English made me complicit in perpetuating these perspectives. For example, I recall regularly encouraging students to speak only English at school and celebrating a choral chant the ESL teachers had taught them in which the teacher would enthusiastically ask, "What language do we speak at school?!" and the students would chorally respond "English!" Then they would ask, "And what language do we speak at home?!" and the students would respond, "My language!" I have thought about this a lot, particularly as I began developing a more expansive perspective of language and dynamic educational environments. The limiting perspectives of language that the teachers and I imposed upon children did not accurately represent the ways that real people, including myself and the students with whom I worked, use language in our lives.

Kate's Story

My identity in school was a lot like the majority of my classmates'. I was born and raised in the United States, in a suburb of New York City, and English was my dominant language. I am white, and was raised in an upper-middle-class home. Though I am Jewish, which was not the norm in my hometown, I was neither celebrated nor overtly bullied because of it. A part of me that was different, however, was that my mother was an immigrant. And though she assimilated into American life and the English language, Italian was part of the linguistic and cultural landscape of my home.

Though I heard it my whole life, my mother did not speak Italian with me. When I was young, I didn't think much about it, but as I grew older, I resented what I missed. Despite my inability to speak Italian, my upbringing in a not-quite-monolingual home taught me that what you knew about someone in school wasn't their full story. Though these understandings informed my work with MLs, they did not keep other, more deficit-oriented beliefs from emerging when I became a teacher.

After volunteering at a rural orphanage and primary school in Central America, I began teaching high school English to multilingual learners in New York City. I loved the work, but I also became aware of, and uncomfortable with, the beliefs that surfaced about my students. For one, they used language in ways that differed from my own understanding of bilingualism. Because my mother's Italian was spoken only with our Italian-speaking family, I did not grow up hearing the kind of linguistic mixing demonstrated by my students. I also remembered stories my mother and grandparents would tell, with pride, about how quickly she learned English and blended in with her American classmates. In contrast, my students struggled with grade-level work in English, which my colleagues and I chalked up to differences between "social" or "playground" English and "academic" English. We also attributed their struggles to a "lack of academic literacy" in their home languages.

Such "struggles" stood in contrast to other things I saw in my English classroom. Groups of students used Spanish to analyze Shakespeare's *A Midsummer Night's Dream.* They wrote complex bilingual poetry and journal entries about their lives. I listened to their jokes, stories, complaints, and observations, all told through the fluid, creative, seamless use of their languages. I found myself experiencing cognitive dissonance: how could these students possibly be framed – by standardized tests or by me, their teacher – as "lacking" language and literacy?

After I left full-time teaching and entered graduate school, I came across theories that shed light on these dissonances as well as on my own upbringing. I also met mentors and colleagues, many of whom were bi/multilingual women of color who identified as immigrants and children of immigrants, who told stories of their own families and childhood experiences. I began to reframe not only the "problems" I had once perceived in my students, but also my own internalized narratives about immigration and bilingualism and about my mother and myself.

How Do Our Roots Form and Shape Our Advocacy Work?

Now that we've introduced ourselves and parts of our backgrounds and experiences, we will use them to highlight three central points about our roots and the role they play in critical advocacy work. We believe that our roots:

1. Are shaped by complex, intersecting elements of our identities;
2. Respond to the contexts in which they grow, which include dominant beliefs and ideologies; and
3. Expand through alternative experiences and counter-narratives that challenge and resist dominant beliefs.

As we discuss each of these beliefs, we'll revisit elements of our own stories. While you'll be invited to reflect more intentionally at the end of the chapter, we encourage you to begin considering your own stories – how you have been rooted and how your roots have expanded over the course of your life and career.

Our Roots Are Shaped by Intersecting Elements of Our Identities

Voices From the Field

> I see a lot of myself as a child in these kids, and I think it definitely helps me do the type of advocacy that I do. I see them, and I see little me struggling in an English-dominant country, not knowing the language. I want to be the teacher that I needed when I was little. And so I always strive to be that person. I was in a very white community, English-dominant, no one spoke Spanish. I never even got official multilingual instruction. So it really does shape what I do now. I feel like it's very much who I am.
>
> – Martha, Spanish–English Dual Language teacher, Kentucky

Our identities are formed by both social forces and personal experiences. Some elements of our identities, such as race, ethnicity, cultural background, nationality or tribal affiliation, sex, gender, sexual orientation, class, age, and dis/ability, often root us in different social groups, helping us find spaces where those aspects of our identities can be protected and bolstered. Very few of us belong to only one social group; instead, our multiple social identities intersect and overlap in ways that create more complex identities, some of which are shaped and contested by dynamics of power and privilege (Crenshaw, 1989, 1991).

In Kate's story, we see how elements of her identity, like race and class, intersect with elements like language, ethnicity, and culture. Important elements of Kate's identity (being the child of an immigrant mother; being Jewish; having a language other than English in her home) remained out of sight, in large part because of her whiteness, her upper-middle-class-ness, and her language practices, which all aligned with "the norm" of her peers and community. For Rebecca, language, ethnicity, and culture also intersected with her racial and classed identity. Though she was rooted in Peruvian and Cuban culture, her upbringing in a predominantly white, monolingual community in Kentucky and attendance at English-medium schools relegated these ethnolinguistic roots to her "home" life. Though these roots were not highlighted in school, Rebecca's ethnic and racial background still shaped her experiences. When she started identifying outwardly as Latina, for example, she noticed that some of her teachers made assumptions about what part of town she was from and what nationalities her parents were, affiliating Latine identity with a lower socioeconomic status and assuming all Latines were Mexican.

Other elements of our identities, like our work, traditions and customs, hobbies, interests, personality traits, and family dynamics and roles, are unique to our own individual experiences. Depending on time and context, different aspects of these highly personal identities may rise to the surface or stay out of view. As we go through our lives and our social networks and experiences expand, so too do our identities, as they adapt and modify aspects of who we are. As illustrated in the preceding Voices from the Field quote, Martha's individual experience of being a multilingual learner in a white, English-dominant community is an integral element of her roots, grounding her in advocacy she felt she did not receive as a child.

In Rebecca's story, the dynamics of her own family – her parents' simultaneous pride in their culture and language and the practice of speaking mostly English with their children despite it not being their own home language – played a role in how she chose to identify (or not) in school. Kate's job as a teacher became an important part of her identity, reshaping what she thought she knew about language and being a student in school. For both of us, our own unique family dynamics and practices shaped how we entered our professional work with multilingual learners. That work, in turn, continues to help us interpret our own individual identities and the affordances, oversights, and ways of thinking they brought about in us.

Who we are is not static; while our roots are shaped by social categories, social forces, and our own personal traits and experiences, they also shift in response to new people, situations, information, and experiences. In this way, our root systems are highly complex, made up of the various strands of our intersecting identities that define (and redefine) who we are in our lives and in our work with MLs.

Our Roots Respond to the Contexts in Which They Grow, Which Includes Dominant Beliefs and Ideologies

Voices From the Field

I'm not bilingual. I'm white, female, just like, typical. I ask myself sometimes, like, why am I so passionate about this? In no way does this come close to being anything I was raised with. I went to very monolingual schools, like we had no ethnic diversity in our school. . . . My parents are very unkind to people who do not speak English and say a lot of negative things. It's very off-putting. They truly don't understand what I do or why I do it.

– Tammy, former English Learner teacher and current elementary school Vice Principal, California

The beliefs and ideologies that forge dominant understandings of language, culture, teaching, and learning influence the growth of our roots. Particularly for those of us who work with racialized MLs, we must be aware of how our roots have been shaped by ideologies that cast these students as deficient and lacking (Flores & Rosa, 2015; García et al., 2021). For example, many of us have been socialized to affiliate characteristics and traits such as home language/accent, surname, or phenotypical appearance with being "non-white," a process that *racializes* – and thus further marginalizes – MLs. Some have argued that this racialization process is structurally reinforced by language-focused programs that "separate and marginalize [MLs] relative to white students and spaces of Whiteness" (Ghast et al., 2022, p. 1012). Recognizing that our roots were forged amidst racist, classist, monolingual, and xenophobic ideologies and discourses is integral to understanding the deepest parts of ourselves. As Tammy said, though she is passionate about working with MLs, she acknowledges that her whiteness and monolingualism, her ethnically homogenous upbringing, and her own parents' bias toward non-English speakers are important parts of her story.

Rebecca's embarrassment about her family's use of Spanish and her father's accented English, as well as her initial resistance to formally learning Spanish in school, is rooted in dominant notions about what it means to be American and about the power of English (Lippi-Green, 2012). Ideologies that make "native" and "unaccented" English central to notions of national identity (Shuck, 2009) and individual capability and intelligence (Thorstensson Dávila, 2013) are similar to those that shaped Kate's recollections of her mother's stories about her schooling. Her mother's pride in assimilating quickly into her American school, speaking English so well that she "passed" as a native speaker, and outperforming her English-speaking peers, forged Kate's perceptions of what it meant to be a "good immigrant" as well as a good student.

These dominant beliefs and ideologies have inevitably shown up in our own work with MLs. Kate's internalized raciolinguistic ideologies (Flores & Rosa, 2015), or beliefs about language and race that influence how we perceive and judge different languages and language varieties based on racial characteristics, led to the belief that her MLs had only "social," not "academic," language. And even though she herself does not speak her mother's language, Kate equated what she saw as her students' lack of competence in their home languages with their struggles in school. Rebecca's own English-medium schooling and the seemingly natural separation of her "home" and "school" language practices led her to view English-medium programs as most effective for helping multilingual learners become acclimated to schooling in the US. Though these kinds of monoglossic ideologies (García, 2009; García & Torres-Guevara, 2009), which assert that students should learn and use only "standard English," most certainly led to her own internalized linguistic oppression (Freire, 1970), they also shaped Rebecca's approach to working with immigrant and refugee youth in ways that she now recognizes were oppressive.

As we stated in our discussion of the political elements of our work with MLs, recognizing how discourses and ideologies negatively impact our students is integral to critical advocacy. Thus, recognizing how such ideologies exist and have shaped our *own* roots, and how those roots have shaped our beliefs and actions in our personal lives and our work, is essential for critical advocates.

Our Roots Expand Through Alternative Experiences and Counter-narratives That Expand and Challenge Us

Voices From the Field

> In my second year teaching, I had a group of ELL students in my class, and I realized immediately, "Oh, my goodness, they need something different from me." And so that was the beginning. And from that point on, I just knew that I had to do things differently. I had to think differently. I had to plan differently. Thank God, it was [only] my second year because it impacted my entire trajectory.
>
> – Grace, Director of World Languages and English as a New Language, New York

While it is important to understand the ways that deficit-oriented beliefs and ideologies shape our roots, it is equally important to understand how alternative experiences and counter-stories, or the narratives of marginalized people and communities told from their own perspectives (Delgado, 1989; Solórzano & Yosso, 2002), also shape our roots. Critical advocates gain access to such stories and perspectives in many ways, both planned (i.e., forging relationships with people unlike themselves, living and working in diverse communities, engaging with media that contain alternative points of view) and unplanned (i.e., as in Kate's story or in the preceding Voices from the Field quote, finding themselves in personal and professional settings that challenge their preconceptions and being open to change).

Both Rebecca and Kate's roots expanded through their relationships with bilingual, immigrant/immigrant origin students. In Kate's work as a classroom teacher and Rebecca's work in an after-school program, we saw the sophisticated ways that students navigated their schooling and their worlds despite the deficit-oriented labels, policies, and programs that defined their educational experiences. Rather than relegate their languages and cultures to one place or time – as both Rebecca and Kate had been raised and socialized to do – students engaged in what we would later learn in graduate school was termed translanguaging (García, 2009). As students mixed and meshed and drew on all of their linguistic resources to learn, they resisted the ideologies that defined what was "academic language" and *who* was a "good student" (García et al., 2021).

In addition to learning about translanguaging and other asset-based perspectives on MLs, graduate school invited both Rebecca and Kate to look back at their own roots through alternative framings. When Rebecca learned about bilingual education, which she and her parents had not known existed, she rethought the schooling options she had access to in Kentucky and the limited opportunities students continue to have there today. When Kate heard her intelligent, successful mentors' and colleagues' stories about growing up bilingual in the US, "struggling" in similar ways to the students she taught, she began to consider whether these "struggles" emerged due not to individual "problems" but to the linguistically and culturally subtractive schooling (Valenzuela, 1999) MLs endure.

Both Rebecca and Kate also reconsidered feelings they had about their own linguistic practices and identities. Rebecca recalls that she resisted identifying as "bilingual" because she couldn't express herself in Spanish the *exact* way she could in English; a translanguaging perspective showed her that this was typical, and that the ideal "balanced bilingual" was merely a manifestation of monoglossic ideologies. Similarly, Rebecca's work with multilingual youth who spoke so clearly about how they used language helped her understand that even as a child, she, too, was strategic about how she used language. For Kate, her own shame in not speaking her mother's language changed as she contextualized her mother's experience in broader understandings of immigration and assimilation and reframed her own languaging through an asset-based lens. By thinking about education through linguistically and culturally sustaining approaches (Paris & Alim, 2017), Kate also saw how her mother's and her own schooling might have been different, resulting in integration, rather than siloing, of their linguistic and cultural identities.

Roots: Anchoring and Expanding Our Critical Advocacy

An understanding of roots as both anchors *and* persistent catalysts for expansive growth is integral to our discussion of critical advocacy. We cannot discount the roots that grew in the formative years of our lives. These roots, which are shaped by our multifaceted, intersectional identities and by dominant beliefs and ideologies, are integral to understanding the *personal* element of critical advocacy, or the ways that our backgrounds and experiences shape who we are and how we enter our work with MLs. With that said, we also emphasize the perpetual and expansive rooting that occurs as we respond to our changing contexts and understandings. Understanding roots in this way ties the personal to the *political* element of critical advocacy; as we expand our root systems, we see beyond ourselves and beyond the individual level to how powerful sociopolitical forces flow through the systems that shape us. It also ties both the personal and the political to the *pedagogical*. If we see part of critical advocacy as constantly growing our awareness of both our complicity in and agency to work against deficit-oriented ideologies, policies, and practices, then we can be more thoughtful and realistic about our efforts in classrooms and schools.

Digging In: Exploring Your Roots

We now invite you to delve into your own roots through the following guided writing/composing activity. For each of the three stages of reflection, jot down, draw/doodle, or otherwise represent your thinking. Ideally, this activity should be done with others who are learning about critical advocacy alongside you, but it can also be done independently.

1. Think about elements of your identity that have shaped your roots and relate to your work with MLs. You can consider:
    - Which aspects of your identity were recognized or celebrated at school and which were disregarded or suppressed? How does this compare to the experiences of the MLs with whom you work?
    - Were your identities reflected in your schooling (i.e., in the curriculum, your teachers, the language of instruction, etc.)? Which, if any, were not?
    - Which aspects of your identity most shape your approach to working with MLs? In what ways?
2. Reflect on your internalized perceptions of and/or common discourses around MLs. Think about how you have come to those beliefs and how the elements of your identity that you wrote about relate to your existing perceptions. You can reflect on:
    - What images come to mind when you think of MLs?

- What messages have you received (i.e., from family, media, colleagues, etc.) about MLs, their families, and linguistically diverse communities?
- How would you describe conversations about MLs in your professional context? What discourses do you commonly hear?

3. Think about your own alternative experiences with counter-narratives and/or non-dominant perceptions of MLs. You can use these questions to guide your reflection:
   - When have your pre-existing perceptions/ beliefs about MLs been disrupted? How and why did they change?
   - Have any of your personal and/or professional relationships (re)shaped your perceptions of MLs?
   - Have you ever attempted to disrupt dominant perceptions/narratives about MLs? What was the result? What did you learn?
4. Exchange reflections with others and/or re-read your own writing/composition. What did you learn about yourself? Did anything come up that surprised you? What will you do with the information you gained through this exercise?

Conclusion

As critical anti-racist educator Tricia Ebarvia (2019) says, "The internal work matters a lot. You cannot disrupt if you don't understand how systems of oppression work. You cannot understand how systems of oppression work until you come to terms with how they have worked on you." Understanding what has shaped our roots and how our roots are constantly in a state of growth and change is integral to critical advocacy. In this chapter, we shared our stories about who and what have shaped our roots. We laid out the three beliefs that inform our understanding of the roots of critical advocacy, including how they are shaped by our complex identities, by the dominant beliefs and ideologies that circulate about MLs, and by the alternative experiences and counter-narratives we encounter throughout our lives. We also invited you to delve beneath the surface and explore your own roots in order to better understand what has both grounded and expanded you and your work with MLs. In Chapter 2, we'll dig deeper into the political elements of critical advocacy roots: our awareness and unlearning of deficit-oriented ideologies about MLs, their families, and their communities.

 Critical Advocacy Action Planning Connection

What can you take from this chapter's discussion of **roots** into your critical advocacy action planning? You might think about how:

- **Our roots shape what we care about.** Before engaging in any tangible critical advocacy work, you might consider why the issue or question you've identified resonates with you. How did you come to identify it, and why does it matter?
- **Our roots influence what we perceive to be just or unjust.** There are many, many inequalities in schools. Part of critical advocacy action is being transparent about what we are choosing to take action about and why. How do your roots potentially shape your interpretations of what is just or unjust?
- **Our roots never stop growing.** Though our prior lived experiences influence our critical advocacy work, we can always expand our perspectives to make our actions more meaningful, sustainable, and effective. How can you expand your perspectives throughout your critical advocacy action?

2

Ideologies and Beliefs About Advocacy

The roots of our critical advocacy efforts respond to the contexts in which they grow, meaning they are inherently shaped by the ideologies and beliefs that permeate our contexts. Deficit-oriented ideologies about multilingual learners (MLs), which perpetuate views of MLs as "lacking" or "behind," are pervasive; they are infused into teacher training programs, shape instructional and programming decisions, and circulate in everyday discourse used to describe MLs, their families, and communities (Accurso et al., 2019). In this chapter, we explore common framings of advocacy with the goal of unpacking the ideologies embedded in them. In doing so, we emphasize that while traditional framings of advocacy may reflect good intentions at the individual level, they can perpetuate the belief that those with certain racial, ethnic, ability, and linguistic capital are the only ones who can navigate inequitable systems *on behalf of* those with less capital.

We highlight that an integral aspect of being a critical advocate is engaging in the hard work of uncovering the ideologies that shape our roots and inform our approach to advocacy. By interrogating our own beliefs with eyes wide open to the ideologies, structures, and biases that shape common perceptions of, and approaches to working with, MLs and their families. We close by offering alternative orientations that illustrate how critical

DOI: 10.4324/9781003628774-4

advocates can resist deficit-oriented approaches to advocacy, instead grounding their efforts in strength-based perspectives and the voices, knowledge, and leadership of MLs and their communities.

Deficit-Oriented Framings of Advocacy

Deficit-oriented framings of advocacy often position those who identify as advocates as socially and morally responsible for advocating *for*, rather than in partnership *with*, those positioned as "unable" to speak for themselves due to their marginalized status. Thus, advocates moving from this perspective feel called to speak for those who are oppressed, or to be the "voice for the voiceless." While likely grounded in good intentions, this kind of advocacy can further disadvantage marginalized populations by framing the injustices they experience as individual experiences rather than as structural disadvantages imposed upon them. Such a perspective positions marginalized populations as powerless while perpetuating the belief that MLs and their families lack the ability to make informed decisions by and for themselves.

In addition to erasing the structural nature of systems of oppression, deficit-oriented framings of advocacy often place the advocate, rather than those experiencing marginalization, at the center of the work. This is similar to Picower's (2012) description of deficit-oriented teaching as a "Here I Come to Save the Day!" mentality. Critical advocacy draws attention to the inadvertent sidelining of members of the marginalized communities that advocates seek to support, thus erasing these individuals' voices, their own advocacy efforts, and, at times, their actual needs.

Embedded in such an approach to advocacy is a savioristic framing of MLs as helpless or voiceless, waiting to have help handed to them. Such a framing fails to acknowledge the strengths and bodies of knowledge that MLs and their families possess and instead positions them as lacking in school-valued and -aligned bodies of knowledge. Noguera (2009) referred to this phenomenon as the "pobrecito syndrome," which he used to describe teachers who feel sorry for students from marginalized backgrounds and over-empathize in ways that lower their expectations. While some may see these lowered expectations and other "modifications" (e.g., allowing students to "opt out" of certain activities; assigning remedial worksheets instead of grade-level materials) as coming from a place of empathy and compassion, critical advocacy emphasizes empathy from a critical and action-oriented perspective. In other words, we emphasize that advocates can both feel for and center MLs' needs *and* recognize their strengths and potential for meeting high academic standards and expectations.

Digging In: Exploring Deficit-Oriented Ideologies and Policies

Watch the short film "Immersion" about the experiences of a 10-year-old student, Moises, and his teacher after the passing of Proposition 227, the "English for the Children" initiative that made bilingual education illegal in California.

- What ideological perspectives or beliefs do you see in the approach Moises's teacher takes to advocating for him? In the principal's response to the teacher?
- Do you see the pobrecito syndrome manifesting in either party's actions?
- How does the state-level policy and context shape the teacher's approach to advocacy?
- What is the interplay of state-level policy, deficit-oriented ideology, and advocacy in this short film?

While traditional framings of advocacy may, on the surface, appear to reflect good intentions, they often remain steeped in the false notion that there are two distinct parties: those who possess the skills, power, and privilege necessary for engaging in advocacy work (i.e., the "advocate") and those who lack such skills and therefore require the "help" of those more fortunate (i.e., the "recipient" of advocacy efforts). A critical advocacy perspective rejects such a hierarchical perception of advocacy, instead calling on advocates to work toward leveling the playing field by digging deeper into who we are and how we locate ourselves and our beliefs in the work. In the process, we can come to recognize how ideologies shape who we are, what we believe, and what we do. Only by engaging in such a reflective process can we engage in advocacy efforts that are meaningful, sustainable, and effective.

Countering Deficit-Oriented Framings of Advocacy

Critical advocacy calls on educators to interrogate our own beliefs, critique our own practices, and unlearn the deficit-oriented ideologies that may be embedded in those beliefs and practices. In doing so, we work toward understanding how the injustices MLs and their families face are rarely the result of individual efforts (or a lack thereof). Rather, they stem from larger structural inequities, perpetuated through everyday actions, that shape the learning experiences of MLs. For example, rather than view a lack of participation on the part of MLs' families as evidence of a lack of interest in their children's schooling, critical advocates might investigate the cultural and linguistic norms of the school. In this way, critical advocacy refuses to locate "problems" within MLs themselves or to "solve" those "problems" through practices that further marginalize them. Instead, critical advocates focus on embracing the difficult work of uncovering and working to shift the structures and policies that systematically lead to inequitable schooling experiences for MLs and the structural exclusion of their families.

As critical advocates, we cannot critique systems and structures affecting MLs without unpacking how we have benefited from them. For example, in Chapter 1, we engaged in critical self-reflection of our own roots, acknowledging how we may have perpetuated deficit-oriented perspectives of multilingualism and MLs in our own work. By engaging in this honest critical self-reflection, we can begin to de-center ourselves, reflect on our own biases, and consider what it means to engage ethically in advocacy efforts in our local contexts. Such practices are essential for reframing how educators understand and engage in advocacy, viewing MLs not as pobrecitos in need of help, but as resourceful individuals whose linguistic and cultural capital should be viewed as a strength and an asset.

Similarly, critical advocacy is grounded in asset- and community-oriented perspectives of MLs, their families, and the bodies of knowledge and skills that they bring to their learning. For example, González et al. (2005) have called on educators to recognize that MLs possess "funds of knowledge" derived from lived experiences that can contribute to their schooling. They highlighted the use of funds of knowledge as a resource for enhancing students' academic learning and called on teachers to explore their students' lives outside of school to better understand their needs as well as their rich familial and community inheritances. When critical advocates operate from such a perspective, they can promote culturally sustaining approaches (Paris & Alim, 2017) that do not just support but actively seek to grow students' linguistic repertoires, cultural identities, and content knowledge. From this perspective, then, critical advocacy is framed as a form of active resistance to the common subtractive schooling practices (Valenzuela, 1999) that have historically ignored or attempted to rid MLs of their vast bodies of knowledge and linguistic skills.

At the same time, critical advocates recognize that the education of MLs is not politically neutral; our efforts are always entangled with systems of power that shape every aspect of the work we do. Dominant deficit-oriented ideologies about MLs and their languaging practices are particularly pervasive, reinforced by mainstream society and many educators' views that position monolingualism and privilege standard English as the norm and expectation (García, 2009; García & Torres-Guevara, 2009). Thus, the work of critical advocacy involves not only shifting practices for MLs but also raising awareness of how and why certain languages and their speakers are privileged at the expense of others. In this sense, critical advocacy moves beyond a simple celebration of linguistic diversity to call for heteroglossic perspectives of language (Bakhtin, 1981; García, 2009), recognizing language as expansive and dynamic.

Kate has written extensively about translanguaging, focusing on how schools can make space for *all* of their students' languages at *all* times through rigorous, engaging instruction and assessment (Seltzer et. al., 2025). In designing ways for students to expand their linguistic repertoire (rather than simply learn English) and express their understandings of content through their uniquely multilingual perspectives, teachers can center students' humanity and promote cognitive justice by recognizing their diverse ways of being and knowing (de Sousa Santos, 2018). These seemingly small but ideologically significant shifts can profoundly impact both students and teachers. They help deconstruct the boundaries that position MLs against the ideological norm of what a successful student should look, sound, or behave like (García et al., 2021). Such efforts are central to critical advocacy because they expose and disrupt the power-laden assumptions that marginalize MLs, thereby opening space for more equitable educational possibilities and approaches to advocacy.

Critical advocacy is rooted in the belief that meaningful change is achieved through solidarity, collaboration, partnership, and dialogue. bell hooks (1994) reminds us that lived experience is a form of knowledge, meaning that those who have experienced ongoing oppression are often the ones best equipped to speak about it. Rather than serve as a "voice for the voiceless," critical advocacy calls on educators to ground their efforts in the expressed needs of those experiencing marginalization by centering their knowledge, voices, and leadership efforts. In this way, critical advocacy becomes a practice of redistributing power by centering the lived knowledge of MLs and their communities, affirming their identities, and disrupting deficit narratives that render them voiceless.

Digging In: (Re)defining Advocacy Through a Critical, Asset-Oriented Lens

At the end of the book's introduction, we invited you to brainstorm your own definition of advocacy through four words or short phrases. At this time, we invite you to return to that brainstorm and consider what, if anything, has shifted based on what you have read in this chapter. Reflect on how a critical, asset-oriented lens has evolved your definition of advocacy and include that in your explanation, drawing, or other representation.

Conclusion

A key element of critical advocacy is examining the ideologies that have shaped our perspectives of, and approach to working with, MLs. Deficit-oriented ideologies pervade traditional advocacy efforts and can, despite good intentions, undermine MLs and their own agency. Specifically, they can shutter MLs' potential to advocate for themselves by positioning them as passive recipients of "help" rather than as active participants in their own liberation. In the process, these deficit-oriented perspectives of MLs limit their learning opportunities while also erasing their existing bodies of language and knowledge. Such perspectives also contribute to the sense of isolation many advocates experience because they imply that "the work" belongs to one individual person, rather than recognizing that all critical advocacy actions must be part of larger, collective, and community-driven efforts if they are to be meaningful, sustainable, and effective.

Growing our own understanding of advocacy and the ideologies that flow through it is essential if we want our efforts to be critical and ethical. By learning about who students are and the skills and bodies of knowledge they possess, educators can affirm and build directly upon what students already know and can do. In viewing MLs as experts of their own experience and engaging collaboratively and equitably with them, critical advocates recognize that they, too, have something to learn. Through these experiences, critical advocates' own framings of and approaches to advocacy benefit as their roots continue to expand and grow. In the next chapter, we introduce the "trunk" of the critical advocacy tree, or the core critical advocacy beliefs that directly challenge the deficit-oriented perspectives that can otherwise render advocacy ineffective, unsustainable, and lacking in meaningful connection to MLs' education.

Critical Advocacy Action Planning Connection

What can you take from this chapter's discussion of **ideologies and beliefs** into your critical advocacy action planning? You might think about how:

- **Our beliefs about MLs are shaped by both our roots and our broader contexts.** Our beliefs about MLs are shaped not only by our roots (e.g., cultural backgrounds, lived experiences) but also by our broader contexts (i.e., the communities we belong to, the schools we teach in, and the dominant ideologies that flow through those spaces). What beliefs or ideological forces shape or influence how those in your community perceive MLs, and the expectations held for them? To what extent do they align with your own beliefs?
- **Uncovering the ideological orientations of our beliefs about MLs requires honest and critical reflection on ourselves and our contexts.** We must critically examine how our assumptions, biases, and lived experiences inform how we view language, culture, and identity. Additionally, we must examine how the larger structures shaping the schooling experiences of MLs (i.e., educational policies, institutional practices) perpetuate our biases. How have your own lived experiences shaped your perspectives on and approaches to working with MLs? What elements of MLs' schooling perpetuate their status in the educational system??
- **We can best interrogate our beliefs when we work in community with others.** Being in community with others provides necessary opportunities to see ourselves, our beliefs, and our biases from a new perspective.

Community-oriented reflection also fosters accountability by ensuring our insights translate into informed, responsive, and responsible advocacy efforts. With whom do you consider yourself to be "in community?" Whose perspectives or voices have shaped your beliefs about MLs? How might engaging with others help you better understand your perspectives and beliefs?

3

The Trunk of Critical Advocacy

In Chapter 2, we delved into some common, albeit problematic, framings of advocacy for multilingual learners (MLs). Despite good intentions, versions of advocacy that are informed by even subconscious beliefs that MLs are voiceless or helpless cannot do the necessary work of disrupting the structural marginalization and inequalities that MLs face at school. Chapter 2 also offered some alternative framings of advocacy, which focus attention on empowerment, criticality, and strength-based perspectives on MLs.

This chapter builds on these alternative framings and describes a second element of the critical advocacy tree: the trunk. This strong, sturdy part of the tree represents the core critical advocacy beliefs that inform and support our approaches to critical advocacy. Though you likely have your own unique beliefs that have grown out of your own roots, this chapter lays out three core beliefs that we see as integral to critical advocacy. As you read, we encourage you to think about whether these beliefs resonate with you or help you define how you understand and do advocacy work. We also invite you to expand on these beliefs, defining the strong core of your own critical advocacy.

Core Critical Advocacy Belief #1: Empathy and Compassion Are Central to Advocacy Work With MLs

Empathy and compassion are pillars of educating MLs. The ability to put oneself in another's shoes and to see all people,

DOI: 10.4324/9781003628774-5

especially those unlike ourselves, as equally worthy and capable, is integral to our work. In Chapter 2, we distinguished between empathy and compassion and *sympathy*. Though many MLs have experiences that may bring up feelings of deep sadness or frustration, doing advocacy work from a place of pity can be counterproductive because it may lead to over-accommodation and a lowering of our expectations for students. Instead, we promote a version of empathy and compassion that is critical and action-oriented. When our empathy and compassion are critical, it means we are curious about our own feelings and the roots of those feelings. We might ask ourselves:

- What am I feeling in response to my students' experiences, and where are those feelings coming from?
- How might my emotional response be shaped by dominant ideologies about MLs (and about language, race, immigration, or ability)?
- Are my feelings rooted in my own assumptions about students' lives?

When our empathy and compassion are action-oriented, it means that we focus on how those feelings can be transformative to the educational experiences of MLs. In this way, our empathy and compassion are not defined by "feeling bad" for students, but by taking action that disrupts deficit perspectives and challenges policies and practices that fail to acknowledge students' humanity and potential. To ensure that our empathy and compassion are action-oriented, we might ask ourselves:

- Am I holding high expectations while also acknowledging the challenges students face?
- How am I using my understanding of students' experiences to challenge deficit ideologies in my school or classroom?
- How am I using my role to push for meaningful change?

By asking ourselves such questions and staying critical about feelings of empathy and compassion, we center the humanity of our students. We do not frame them as lacking or sad; we acknowledge the challenges they face, but locate them within systems and discourses that fail to recognize their full humanity and, in fact, *construct* them as less human (García et al., 2021). This kind of empathy and compassion is powerful fuel for action that dissolves the hierarchies that shape MLs' experiences in school and enables us to advocate for MLs.

Voices From the Field

> One of the personal goals I have is trying to help kids become better advocates for themselves. When I started off, I was doing all of it, and I was taking it all on and then taking it all home. Just a few hours ago, a student said, "I'm in computer science, I've got a 0%, I don't know what to do. Can you get me out of the class?" And I said, "Well, it's a little too late for that. Have you talked to [the teacher] to tell him you don't understand?" She said, "I don't know how." And I said, "Okay, I need you to take your phone, use the translator app, and go up to him and use [it] to communicate . . . I know it's scary." And she said, "Well, what happens if he doesn't help me?" I said, "You won't know until you try. So you try." But that's something that, ten years ago, I wouldn't have told a kid. I would have just gone and burned down a door and tried to do it [myself]. But now I realize that the interaction I'm setting up for both [student and teacher] can be powerful. She's going to learn how to ask for what she needs, and [the teacher is] going to learn how to listen to someone who's brave.
>
> – Jenny, English Learner Instructional Specialist, Oklahoma

Though Jenny may once have taken up some of the problematic framings of advocacy that we describe in Chapter 2 (i.e., "a voice for the voiceless"), she has come to see her role as helping students develop their own self-advocacy. Rather than take on their challenges all by herself, which was unsustainable, she works with this student to navigate communication with a teacher. Jenny does not solve the problem *for* her student; she walks the student through what might help them solve it *themselves*. What is also on display, more implicitly, is Jenny's faith in her colleague. It is possible, given how she had to coach her student, that her fellow teacher may struggle to access empathy and compassion for MLs. She does not bash this teacher or "burn down a door." Instead, she frames the potential interaction as an opportunity for this teacher to "learn how to listen" to an empowered student. In short, Jenny's empathy and compassion are more than just feelings; they are the driving force behind her actions.

Core Critical Advocacy Belief #2: Collaboration and Community Building Strengthen Advocacy Work

As we said in Chapter 2, advocates who have seen themselves as the "voice for the voiceless" reflect the beliefs and messaging of our broader society. Media portrayals of educational advocacy often focus on individual (white) teachers and their heroic efforts (Picower, 2012). However, the work of historians, activists, and community organizers has shown that no action or change is ever accomplished alone.

Ironically, such individualistic accounts can make advocacy feel out of reach for educators on the ground. Perhaps you have thought, "I'm only one person, what can I realistically do?" Recognizing the power of collaboration and community can make advocacy more sustainable and keep advocates oriented toward hope. As organizer and educator Mariame Kaba says, "there is always a possibility for transformation, for us having agency. The idea that we're all powerless is not true. We always have some form of power, if not individually, then collectively, as a force" (Baum, 2023, n.p.).

One of the easiest ways to forge critical advocacy through meaningful, engaged collaboration and community-building is by working with fellow educators. As we saw in the preceding

Voices from the Field quote, this means moving away from the idea that you are the only one who can help MLs and embracing the possibility that our colleagues are or could be on the same page. Cultivating relationships with fellow educators does more than simply amplify advocacy efforts; being in community supports us as human beings.

Voices From the Field

> It is critical for me to have a partner . . . I have to find where I am loved because it helps drive me to be able to do the work.
>
> – Stephanie, English Language Development teacher, Maryland

If advocates do not feel loved, worthy, confident, or supported, their advocacy efforts may be built on a shaky foundation. As Stephanie indicates, seeking fellowship with those around you is an important step in establishing sustainable advocacy. Here are a few ways we have seen educators collaborate with one another to make meaningful change for MLs:

- The CUNY-NYSIEB (City University of New York-New York State Initiative on Emergent Bilinguals) project partnered researchers and teacher educators with schools across the state that served large numbers of MLs. With the support of the research team, schools formed teams made up of teachers, counselors, coaches, parent coordinators, and administrators, among others. These teams identified concrete ways to improve the experiences and outcomes of students. They also brought like-minded educators together to support one another and collaborate to solve their own problems (to read more about these teams, see Sánchez & Menken, 2020).
- Many educators we spoke to participated in collaborative, teacher-led initiatives that supported MLs. From

book clubs to professional learning communities to home visits to partnerships with community organizations and activists, these educators worked together to tap into each other's expertise, expand their knowledge base, and apply their learning to better serve MLs.

- Rita Kohli and her colleagues (2015) discuss the power of teacher-led "critical professional development" (CPD) for justice-minded teachers and teachers of color who are often pushed out of teaching. In a series of case studies, Kohli et al. detail how CPDs are "designed to provoke cooperative dialogue, build unity, provide shared leadership, and meet the critical needs of teachers" (p. 11). These CPDs enabled like-minded educators to collectively "develop their critical consciousness, teach with critical pedagogy, and challenge inequity across schools, districts and policy" (p. 21).
- With the support of a local university professor, two Spanish teachers at a suburban high school in New Jersey partnered to create a student voice project (Brasof, 2015), which engaged a small group of students, including several MLs, in action research to address issues that affected them at school. The teachers and students collaboratively presented their findings and action plans to the district's school board.

While collaboration with colleagues in the school building is important and necessary, connecting with students' communities beyond the walls of the school is also highly important. As Campano et al. (2016) write, "There are innumerable day-to-day examples of educational advocacy that may be invisible to educators, especially if they have little genuine exposure to the neighborhoods and communities of their students" (p. 128). Reaching outside the walls of the school can serve as a powerful reminder of how communities have always supported and educated their own (Cooper et al., 2005). And because immigrant communities are perceived as being less involved in their children's schooling (Valdés, 1996), tapping into and supporting the community-based education and advocacy work that is already happening is a powerful way to both challenge our own implicit bias and expand our efforts in ways that holistically support MLs.

In addition to collaborating and building community with colleagues, critical advocates recognize the importance of working with those at the apex of top-down systems, from building principals to superintendents to school boards. Navigating systems of power and understanding the inner workings of decision-making can be difficult, since many of these systems are opaque by design. And recognizing that the people who make the decisions very often know little about MLs can be frustrating and tedious. However, developing meaningful relationships with these decision-makers and approaching them from a place of cooperation can create important pathways for advocacy. For example, Multilingual Learner teacher Tami from South Carolina found that when she became the state's Teacher of the Year, she suddenly had access to "higher-ups" in the world of education.

Voices From the Field

I'm not afraid to speak my mind, and I'm not afraid to stand up for my students. And a lot of times when you're talking about higher-ups in districts, they don't know, because they're so far removed from the classroom. But you'll find that they're willing to have conversations. Never would I have tried that in my first or second year. Like I would have looked at [the superintendent] like a celebrity, like, I'm not gonna walk up and talk to him. But having been in a smaller setting with those people, and realizing that yeah, they're super busy, and sometimes they might not answer email, but it doesn't mean I'm not gonna try. . . . You have to be willing to do that. There are some things that just aren't right.

– Tami, Multilingual Learner teacher, South Carolina

Though "higher-ups" like superintendents are certainly busy and big picture-oriented, they are not, as Tami realized, "celebrities." Pushing past discomfort or frustration and finding the ear of decision-makers – at any level – is yet another way to collaboratively expand our advocacy efforts in ways that are critically aware of power and influence.

Digging In: Resources for Community-Building

Many advocacy organizations recommend "mapping" activities that enable advocates to build relationships, find allies, and tap into what already exists in their community. For example, the Southern Poverty Law Center recommends community asset-mapping, which "spotlights methods of tapping into the hidden wealth of knowledge in all communities for the benefit of children" (2012). When approaching work with those Tami referred to as "higher-ups," the National Education Association (NEA) recommends power mapping, which can help you "identify who has power in the community, and to figure out what will move those individuals or institutions to do whatever it is you want them to do" (2023).

Core Critical Advocacy Belief #3: Perpetual Learning Is Key to Evolving Our Beliefs, Practices, and Advocacy Efforts

In Chapter 1, we discussed how the roots of the critical advocacy tree are constantly expanding through alternative experiences and counter-narratives. This understanding of roots means that our advocacy efforts and our understandings of *ourselves* are constantly evolving. We grow in these ways when we position ourselves not as having all the answers, but as perpetual learners committed to maintaining curiosity about ourselves, our contexts, our students, and our own advocacy efforts. Alternative experiences and counter-narratives, or stories that complicate those traditionally heard, don't always fall into our laps. In our discussions with critical advocates, we heard about how they actively seek out such perspectives in a variety of ways. Here are just a few:

- Many of the teachers we spoke with had explored diverse roles within the education system. Some pursued administrators' licenses. Others took on mentoring responsibilities. Some left full-time classroom teaching to become coaches, expanding their ability to work with other educators and shape practice. Others remained in the classroom and volunteered to participate in Equity and Inclusion Councils, Parent Advisory Committees, Curriculum Committees, and other school-based advisory groups. Each of these pathways required time and energy but opened opportunities to learn and develop broader understandings of the educational and advocacy landscape for MLs.
- Despite being a veteran teacher with 30 years' experience, Tami, the teacher from South Carolina, visits her colleagues' classrooms, particularly those early in their careers. These intervisitations keep her perspective fresh and enable her to learn from her peers.
- Another veteran teacher, Minerva from Washington, who previously taught in California, utilized her professional organization to learn more about decision-making related to MLs. Though she had attended CABE's (California Association of Bilingual Education) Dual Language institutes in the past, she decided to find out what kind of professional development administrators had access to through the organization. At the next CABE conference, she sought out administrator-facing sessions. Not only did she get to hear what kind of advice administrators were receiving from CABE, but she saw just how few bilingual Latines like her were principals and supervisors.
- Katie, an ESL teacher from Colorado, constantly seeks out opportunities to grow her empathy and understanding of her students. She has read books like *Solito: A Memoir* by Javier Zamora alongside her colleagues. She participated in an organized trip to the border in El Paso. She engages

in critical, sometimes uncomfortable, conversations with family and friends about immigration.

Each of the preceding examples illustrates that perpetual learning can be simultaneously personal, political, and pedagogical. Working with MLs and committing to critical advocacy means cultivating curiosity and openness to new information and experiences. Whether that involves asking questions of yourself and your roots, reading literature and consuming media that expand your understanding of the political context and rhetoric shaping the education of MLs, or trying out new pedagogical approaches and tools, perpetual learning deepens critical advocacy.

Conclusion

This chapter described the three core critical advocacy beliefs that make up the trunk of our tree: empathy and compassion are central to advocacy with MLs, collaboration and community-building strengthen advocacy work, and perpetual learning evolves our advocacy efforts. Strong beliefs and convictions strengthen our core so that our advocacy *actions* – the branches, off-shoots, and leaves of our tree, which we explore next in Part II of the book – are meaningful, sustainable, and effective for MLs. Hopefully, as you read about these three core critical advocacy beliefs, you also thought about what unique beliefs you bring with you into your work. The trunk of your own critical advocacy efforts, which grows out of your ever-expanding root system, is something we hope you'll continue to explore throughout the book.

 Critical Advocacy Action Planning Connection

What can you take from this chapter's discussion of the **trunk** into your critical advocacy action planning? You might think about how:

- **Our trunk helps us respond to problematic framings of MLs and of advocacy.** The three core beliefs we describe in this chapter provide a contrast to deficit-oriented thinking about MLs and about advocacy. They invite critical questions about your own advocacy actions, which can help root them in strength-based perspectives, such as: what assumptions might I be making about the question or issue I've identified? Who have I involved in my planning, and who might be missing? Have I learned enough about who is already doing this work and what resources already exist?

- **Our trunk shapes how we approach critical advocacy action.** There is no one way to engage in advocacy work. However, we argue that advocacy guided by empathy and compassion, collaboration and relationships, and perpetual learning is most meaningful, sustainable, and effective. As you consider action, you might get curious about: which of the three core beliefs we describe as the trunk come naturally to me, and which are challenging, and why? How does the ease or difficulty I have with any of these beliefs shape my approach to advocacy action?

Part II

Extending the Branches and Sprouting Off-Shoots and Leaves of Critical Advocacy

Part II of the book moves into the *actions* that emerge from our critical advocacy beliefs. With that said, we encourage you to keep coming back to the roots and trunk of your work, explored in depth in Part I. Understanding your roots means understanding how the terrain of your upbringing and early experiences has shaped their growth as well as how those same roots have continued to grow and expand over time. Understanding your trunk means understanding the beliefs that make up the core of your advocacy work with multilingual learners (MLs).

Without curiosity and criticality about the roots and trunk of our tree, it is possible for our advocacy actions to fall into some of the deficit-oriented patterns we described in Chapter 2. For example, without examining our own biases, well-intentioned advocacy may be rooted in pity or low expectations for MLs. Without an asset-based, community-oriented mindset, advocacy action may manifest as a "hero's mission" – not lacking in passion, perhaps, but certainly lacking criticality. Your tree's branches, the core areas of critical advocacy action, and its off-shoots and leaves, the small, locally-specific enactments of critical advocacy, can only grow and blossom if they are supported by a strong, well-nourished core and foundation.

Chapter 4 describes four core areas, or branches, of critical advocacy action: pedagogical decision-making, relationship-building and community connections, local policy-making, and disrupting deficit ideologies of MLs. We describe each branch, noting the institutional and ideological barriers that can stand in the way of meaningful change for MLs as well as the ways

DOI: 10.4324/9781003628774-6

advocates navigate those barriers through small, local critical advocacy actions, or what we refer to as the off-shoots and leaves.

When talking about critical advocacy action, it is imperative to do so with eyes wide open. By that, we mean when engaging in critical advocacy for MLs, it is inevitable that you will come up against professional and personal challenges. We discuss these challenges in Chapter 5, not to focus on the negative, but to be honest about critical advocacy work. Such honesty, as well as the self-work, self-care, and community that can sustain us, ensures that our critical advocacy actions are meaningful, sustainable, and ultimately effective for MLs.

4

The Branches, Off-Shoots, and Leaves of Critical Advocacy

Critical advocacy must involve action. And our actions, both the branches that grow from the sturdy trunk of our tree and the off-shoots and leaves that sprout from them, are tied to who we are. While some may thrive organizing campaigns or other large-scale actions on behalf of MLs, others do best when volunteering one-on-one at a refugee resettlement center or piloting a justice-oriented research project with students in the classroom. We urge you to think of critical advocacy action as *any* enactment of your beliefs that positively shapes the experiences of MLs in your context and contributes to educational equity. In this chapter, we describe four branches, or core areas, of critical advocacy action:

- Pedagogical decision-making;
- Relationship-building and community connections;
- Local policy-making; and
- Disrupting deficit ideologies of MLs.

Though there are many branches of action that could be considered critical advocacy, we focus on these four because they have come up consistently in our conversations with advocates for MLs. For each one, we describe the institutional and ideological barriers that often block progress toward meaningful change for MLs. We also highlight how advocates navigate these

DOI: 10.4324/9781003628774-7

barriers through small, local actions – off-shoots and leaves – that help them better serve their students.

Core Critical Advocacy Branch #1: Pedagogical Decision-Making

Barriers to Pedagogical Decision-Making That Supports MLs

Despite the large and growing numbers of MLs in US public schools and the longstanding and robust body of research and scholarship on how to teach them well, the schooling experiences of MLs still leave much to be desired. This is due in large part to deficit-oriented ideologies and discourses that circulate through schools and beyond about MLs' languages and cultures, families and communities, and their perceived ability to learn and be successful. Even in supportive settings, there is a deeply-held belief that learning and "mastering" English (particularly as measured on standardized assessments) is the most important part of MLs' schooling (García & Kleifgen, 2018). The hierarchy of so-called standard, academic English has led to the erasure of students' home languages, the segregation of MLs into what Guadalupe Valdés (2014) called "ESL ghettos," and, relatedly, to an education devoid of intellectual rigor. In other words, the over-emphasis on teaching English through standardized, reductive, disengaging methods and curricula devalues and disregards students' linguistic and cultural knowledge, community wisdom, and lived experiences, as well as the expertise and skills of the teachers trained to work with them.

Aside from those who pursue the teaching of MLs, there is a lack of understanding among educators about what MLs need in school (Lee et al., 2025). As de Jong and Harper (2005) wrote two decades ago, MLs need more than "just good teaching"; *all* educators must be prepared to help MLs learn language through content (Gibbons, 2014) as well as to attend to their social-emotional well-being. And yet, barriers to pedagogical decision-making that support MLs persist in schools. For example, despite our knowledge that, when possible, strong bilingual education is the most effective and supportive way to educate MLs, most are placed in "mainstream" settings and receive only "pull-out" ESL services (Wright, 2025). Despite our understanding that providing students with home language resources, regardless of their program setting, can increase their access to grade-level content (Seltzer et al., 2025), most schools and classrooms remain English-only spaces. And despite the evidence that points to the efficacy of English language teachers' co-teaching and co-planning with content-area teachers (Dove & Honigsfeld, 2017), the time and space to develop this supportive collaborative practice is rarely granted to teachers.

Taking Action: Off-Shoots and Leaves of Pedagogical Decision-Making

Though barriers to pedagogical decision-making that support MLs persist, teaching MLs well is a powerful area of critical advocacy action because it asserts their right to equitable, dignified, and intellectually rich learning. In this section, we feature examples of off-shoots and leaves that sprout from the branch of pedagogical decision-making. We begin with the following quotes from our Voices from the Field interviews:

Voices From the Field

> On a district level, my main focus right now is trying to bring high-quality instruction to students . . . how can we go beyond the fact that [teachers] don't have classroom management issues [with MLs]? I feel like a lot of principals are like, "Oh, it's going great in there." And I'm like, "They're doing coloring worksheets and crosswords in eleventh grade. Tell me how that's going great." So I've been trying to train some of the other instructional coaches so they know what to look for.
>
> – Jenny, EL Instructional Specialist, Oklahoma
>
> For me, advocacy is ensuring that students get access to their curriculum rather than [being] put

> on a Chromebook or do[ing] alternative activities during class. The teachers need to know how to give them access. What accommodations do they need to provide? What types of scaffolds do they need so that these students can access [the curriculum]?
>
> – Tammy, former English Learner teacher and current elementary school Vice Principal, California
>
> When summer curriculum writing happens, I say, you must have an ENL [English as a New Language] teacher [there so] that the curriculum map and projects have all the built-in supports and resources to ensure that they're accessible to ELL students.
>
> – Grace, Director of World Languages and English as a New Language, New York

These educators recognize that there are inequities in how MLs are taught. Jenny highlights that despite a lack of management issues, a classroom where eleventh graders are doing busy work like crosswords and coloring is not "going great"; it's lacking in dignity (Poza, 2021). Tammy asserts that practices that inherently separate MLs from their peers, like being on Chromebooks and doing alternative activities, are not equitable. And Grace's insistence that an ENL teacher be a part of curriculum writing implies that this has not always been the case, leading to an overall lack of access for MLs and a disregard for the expertise of ENL teachers. What is also clear from the preceding quotes is how these advocates voiced their expertise and pedagogical knowledge. Too often, teachers of MLs are deprofessionalized and viewed as "supports" for mainstream and content-area teachers rather than experts in their own right. When teachers and instructional leaders who work with MLs refuse this positioning, they raise the school community's awareness of the presence and needs of MLs. Though it should not be solely their responsibility to inform colleagues and leaders about pedagogical decision-making that supports MLs, doing so with the larger goal of cultivating collective teacher efficacy, or the shared belief that collective action can positively affect student outcomes (Hattie, 2016), is beneficial to students and teachers alike.

Consider the following scenarios, which show how off-shoots and leaves of critical advocacy action can sprout from the branch of pedagogical decision-making:

- A math teacher who works with MLs registers for a professional conference and attends a session on translanguaging, where she learned about instructional strategies that would help her students use all their languages to learn in her English-medium classroom. Inspired, she asked two of her math colleagues to join her in trying out one of those strategies in their teaching. As they implemented the strategy, they shared their experiences, troubleshooted, analyzed student work, and planned out their next steps.
- A media specialist in an elementary school saw the need for culturally and linguistically responsive books that would reach the growing ML population. He decided to curate a collection of multilingual, multicultural literature on the topic of *names* and displayed it in the school's library and media center. He also reached out to classroom teachers to organize read-alouds and explore the possibility of a project in which students shared stories of their own names.
- Two high school ESL teachers noticed a pattern: some of their content-area colleagues were organizing classroom groups that consisted only of MLs. When they asked their colleagues about their reasoning, the teachers explained that they were "differentiating instruction." The ESL teachers noticed, however, that these groups were being given work that was unrelated to whole-class instruction and much less engaging. They spoke to their supervisor about offering a Professional Development on meaningful collaborative work and scaffolding instruction for diverse groups of learners.

Digging In: Pedagogical Decision-Making as Critical Advocacy

Think about what kinds of pedagogical decision-making would support MLs in your context. What needs have you noticed? Could you . . .

- Attend and then "turn-key" a meaningful professional development experience related to MLs to fellow educators?
- Learn about a research-based approach like translanguaging and implement it in instruction alongside colleagues?
- Start a professional learning community on supportive, asset-oriented pedagogies for MLs?
- Supplement scripted curricula and/or adapt standardized assessments in ways that support MLs' learning and engagement?
- Survey ML students to gain insight into their interests, learning preferences, and language practices?

Core Critical Advocacy Branch #2: Relationship-Building and Community Connections

Barriers to Relationship-Building and Community Connections

As we discussed in Chapter 3, a core critical advocacy belief is that collaboration and relationship-building strengthen our efforts. However, as many educators know, there are barriers that stand in the way of enacting this belief in schools. For example, schools are not always welcoming to and supportive of multilingual families and communities. There are many school-based barriers to meaningful collaboration with ML families, including "a deficit perspective, a unidirectional approach to parental involvement, and negative school climate" (Arias & Morillo-Campbell, 2008, p. 8). Deficit perspectives include the assumption that there is a lack of both support and resources, material and otherwise, in MLs' homes and communities. This, in turn, justifies a unidirectional approach to involvement; if families and communities have little to contribute, then their involvement can only occur through school-based (and typically narrow and tokenistic) events and initiatives. A negative school climate, manifested through English-only communication, confusing and opaque policies, and unwelcoming staff, to name only a few, is most certainly a barrier to meaningful community-building and stifles the kind of reciprocal relationships that could lead to collective advocacy for MLs. An overall lack of connection to and knowledge of students' lives and networks outside of school can also reinforce such perspectives (González et al., 2005).

Schools are not always supportive of relationship-building among teachers and other school-based professionals, either. As we stated previously, pedagogical collaboration is integral to the success of MLs. Rather than pull students out, away from their peers, grade-level content, and expert-led instruction, classroom instruction can be co-planned and co-taught by mainstream/content-area teachers and English language teachers (Dove & Honigsfeld, 2017). Similarly, classroom teachers can partner with art, music, and other teachers to design multimodal, culturally sustaining instruction and projects. Educators can also collaborate with support staff who share students' home languages and cultural backgrounds, which not only helps students but can disrupt typical hierarchies and the deprofessionalization of uncertificated staff.

While all these school-based collaborations are powerful, they require protected time and institutional support. As a former high school ELA teacher who co-taught with an ESL teacher, Kate remembers how difficult it was to plan together. Her schedule never aligned with her co-teacher's, which meant they often ended up planning via email or text on their own time. The ESL co-teacher was also often pulled out of the ELA classroom at the last minute to cover for absent teachers or to complete bureaucratic tasks. Such disruptions are barriers to the kind of professional collaboration that meaningfully supports MLs and fail to position English language teachers as the professionals they are.

Taking Action: Off-Shoots and Leaves of Relationship-Building and Community Connections

Making connections to students' families and communities and to other educators within a school community is important to advocacy and to students' *and* teachers' social-emotional well-being. Particularly when so many multilingual communities are under extreme stress, there is an urgent need for actions that transcend the traditional boundaries of school. Consider the following two quotes:

Voices From the Field

I'm a monolingual speaker; I communicate in English only, but I run the parent-teacher home visit program for our school. We go on a lot of home visits, and we bring an interpreter if necessary to get to know our students in a place where they feel more comfortable. It's been a really great way to meet the families and get to know the whole student. It has helped us increase our attendance rates [and] increase parent and family involvement at school. We've got more members in the PTO [Parent-Teacher Organization] who are non-native English speakers. We've got more families coming to school events than we have had in the past. Those are always things that I'm trying to work on – getting families into the school, but also going out to see families in the community.

– Danielle, Language Development Coach, Massachusetts

For the first time ever, we have a higher Nepali-speaking population in two of our grade levels. In our state, if [there are] more than 15 students in the same grade level [who share a home language], you have to have a bilingual class. But it's really hard

> to find a Nepali person with a teaching certificate, so this year we [hired a bilingual aide] and have been calling it a "bilingual experience." He is actually somebody from the Nepali community who's here to help kids. There's a community center which we wouldn't have known about unless we spoke to him. He said they have Nepali classes and so many resources. We didn't know, but it's the perfect place to go and see what's going on [with our kids].
>
> – Dr. Dilini, English as a New Language teacher, New York

Though the two examples highlight different off-shoots and leaves of relationship-building and community connection, they have much in common. The first shows how Danielle's outreach, rooted in her desire to develop reciprocal relationships with her students' families, has had positive effects on school structures like PTOs and daily attendance. Danielle's belief in the importance of families to the school's ability to serve "the whole student" and build on their community cultural wealth (Yosso, 2005) is made actionable through home visits, assisted by an interpreter when necessary. The second quote demonstrates how a connection with a community member opened Dr. Dilini's eyes to resources, like the Nepali community center, that support her students and their families outside of school. Without this relationship, which was a creative response to a shortage of certificated Nepali-speaking teachers, Dr. Dilini would never have learned what she now knows about "what's going on with our kids." Overall, what both these examples demonstrate is how a belief in the humanity and dignity of MLs necessitates action in community with others. To know and forge relationships with ML students, these educators made the effort to know and forge relationships with students' families and communities.

Consider the following scenarios, which show how off-shoots and leaves of critical advocacy action can sprout from the branch of relationship-building and community connections:

- An ESL teacher worked at a school that welcomed many refugee students. In addition to her classroom work, she was very involved with a community-based organization that provided support and resources to recently resettled refugees. To supplement her classroom instruction and create a welcoming environment for these children, she video-recorded elders she knew from the organization who shared her students' home languages as they read stories in those languages. The videos became a part of the teacher's classroom listening center (for more on this scenario, see García et al., 2018).
- A high school math teacher at a school serving a largely Caribbean immigrant population wanted to learn more about the community through the eyes of her students, so she decided to plan and conduct a community walk with them. Not only did she meet local community members and learn about the community's rich resources, but she was also able to integrate data they gathered about local businesses into her mathematics instruction.
- An elementary supervisor heard one of the fifth-grade teachers complaining to a colleague about having an ESL teacher "push in" to his classroom to support an ML in her class. Rather than reprimanding this teacher for feeling this way, she invited him to meet with her individually to talk through what aspects of the experience specifically were frustrating. She then offered to attend their co-planning sessions to support them in collaborating to best meet the student's needs.

Digging In: Relationship-Building and Community Connections as Critical Advocacy

Think about what kinds of relationship-building and community connections would support MLs in your context. What needs have you noticed? Could you . . .

- Learn about and potentially partner with local organizations supporting the ML populations at your school and in your community?
- Design an assignment or activity that would position your students as experts and have them teach you about themselves and their communities?
- Propose a community-building activity (e.g., book club, icebreaker during a staff meeting) that would put English language teachers in conversation with "mainstream" content-area teachers about teaching MLs?

Core Critical Advocacy Branch #3: Local Policy-Making

Barriers to Local Policy-Making

When we think of policy-making, we may think about top-down decisions made by federal- and state-level politicians, school boards, or administrators, many of whom have little knowledge of MLs. While macro-level policy-making is important, and critical advocates can certainly play a role in it, we assert that educators on the ground should view themselves as policymakers in their own right (Menken & García, 2010). Larry Cuban (2025) compares teachers to other "street-level bureaucrats," like police and social workers, who "interpret, amend, and implement decisions handed down by their superiors. And in doing so, they end up making policies for their clients, patients, and students" (n.p.). While "bureaucrat" does not account for the kind of creativity and agency that we see as inherent to educators' decision-making, we agree that the interpretation, amendment, and implementation of top-down policies is itself an act of local policy-making.

Educators who work with MLs are constantly setting local policy. At the classroom level, they may make decisions about what languages students can use, enabling students to draw on their translanguaging, the use of their full linguistic repertoire, to learn or preventing them from doing so. They may decide which elements of a scripted curriculum or standardized assessment should be adapted or adjusted based on their professional expertise and knowledge of their students (Ascenzi-Moreno, 2018). At the school or even district level, educators may look closely at the entry procedures and placement practices for MLs, ensuring that they gain accurate information and use it to place students properly.

Despite their constant engagement in local policy-making, it can be difficult for educators of MLs to make decisions that align with asset-oriented research and practice. This is particularly true now, when federal and state policies explicitly go against such research and practice. The drum beat of English acquisition has organized language education policies around time (i.e., how long it should take an ML to test out of language services) and the performance of so-called "academic" or "standard" English on tests (Flores & Rosa, 2015; Schissel, 2019). Teachers are expected to implement, with full fidelity, scripted curricula that do not always leverage their pedagogical knowledge and expertise with MLs. Rather than adapt to students within them, schools foreground *programs* and the language policies that accompany them (i.e., separation of English and students' home languages in dual language bilingual programs [Sánchez et al., 2018]; the use of only English in English-medium programs [Menken & Sánchez, 2019]). In short, standardization – of language, of knowledge, of curricula, of teaching, of programming – serves as a major barrier for those who wish to assert their agency and make local policy decisions that benefit MLs.

Taking Action: Off-Shoots and Leaves of Local Policy-Making

Despite the top-down policies that shape the education of MLs, there has *always* been courageous, transgressive local policy-making on the ground. And when advocates are empowered to assert their agency and interpret, amend, and implement decisions that are handed down from the top, they are better able to meet the unique local needs of ML students. Take, for example, the case of Danielle, who, despite being in a more liberal state, felt the impact of the national political climate on MLs and their families.

Voices From the Field

> We have unfortunately had a lot of families stop sending their children to school. They're afraid to send their children to school. So as a district, we've changed the way we do things when it comes to absences. We [used to] send truancy officers, but we've stopped doing that in the past couple of weeks because we just want families to feel safe. We've shifted the way that we're handling students who've had chronic absenteeism. We're trying to do a lot more outreach, just get phone contact with somebody [and] explain to them what's going on. More support and encouragement and reassurance.
>
> – Danielle, Language Development Coach, Massachusetts

Harsh immigration enforcement policies have a chilling effect on schools and communities. Though many districts have seen upticks in student absences, Danielle and her school's approach to dealing with this reality navigates federal and state-level policies while reflecting core critical advocacy beliefs. Their local policy-making is clearly rooted in empathy and an understanding of what their students' families face. Rather than look past the sociopolitical realities of their students and treat their absenteeism as simply a disciplinary problem to be handled by truancy officers, they take a different approach. The fact that Danielle and her school did not simply stick to what they've always done and instead shifted their policies as they learned more about their students and families reflects their commitment to perpetual learning and, relatedly, flexibility in their approaches. Local policy-making like this, rooted in compassion, relationality, and responsiveness, is an act of critical advocacy.

Consider the following scenarios, which show how off-shoots and leaves of critical advocacy action can sprout from the branch of local policy-making:

- A middle school Vice Principal created a committee to develop a school language policy. Drawing on language policy research she explored in her graduate program (e.g., Menken & Sánchez, 2019), she led the committee through a discussion of their school's values and how they could be reflected in their treatment of students' diverse languages. The finalized language policy was presented to the whole school community.
- An elementary school teacher shared an article with her grade level team that discussed responsive adaptations (Ascenzi-Moreno, 2018), or shifts in the implementation of informal reading assessments that take MLs' language practices into account. The team read and discussed the article together, ultimately deciding to propose a change in policy that would enable all teachers to deviate from the rigid assessment practices in ways that benefitted MLs.
- A parent coordinator drafted a school-wide communication policy that centered the needs of ML families. The policy included resources and templates that teachers and other educators could use to communicate with families as well as ideas for how to build family engagement and empowerment. He presented a draft of the policy, alongside school leaders, to families of MLs to incorporate their insights and suggestions.

Digging In: Local Policy-Making as Critical Advocacy

Think about what kinds of local policy-making would support MLs in your context. What needs have you noticed? Could you . . .

- Explore existing policy related to discipline, academic performance, etc., to see whether/how MLs' needs and perspectives are included?
- Draw attention to the *lack* of an explicit language policy at your school and propose the development of one?
- Become familiar with how your school identifies and places MLs and compare those to state policy and research-based best practices?

Core Critical Advocacy Branch #4: Disrupting Deficit Ideologies About ML Students

Barriers to Disrupting Deficit Ideologies About MLs

As we have discussed throughout this book, barriers to meaningful advocacy for MLs result from the underlying deficit-oriented ideologies that flow through schools and other institutions. Such ideologies can be difficult to address because, as we explored in Chapter 2, they are often couched in well-meaning sentiments and good intentions. For example, hearing a fellow teacher say that she is "making the curriculum easier" for MLs may indicate that classroom work is being watered down, not made more accessible by differentiation. Being privy to a conversation about how difficult it is to get parents to participate in events due to "cultural differences" may indicate a belief that such differences are a "problem" to solve rather than a situation to navigate with care and confidence in parents' desire to participate in their children's lives. Critical advocates are just that – *critical* – of such discourse, but that awareness does not make scenarios like these any easier to counter.

There are many barriers to intervening when deficit ideologies rooted in racism, classism, xenophobia, or coloniality surface, particularly in schools. For one, schools are filled with people who say they care for MLs and their education. It is rare to find a teacher or other professional who comes right out and says that MLs have less potential to learn or less right to an education than their English-speaking peers. Thus, drawing attention to the deficit-oriented nature of colleagues' discourse can be socially uncomfortable and awkward. We also run the risk of hurting the feelings of people we care about, and who truly care about students. Rather than find creative, caring ways of navigating this discomfort, many educators simply stay silent, and deficit-oriented discourses persist.

In other situations, deficit ideologies are voiced more forcefully and less implicitly. We have heard too many stories of MLs being referred to as "nilingües," "non-nons," or other labels that highlight MLs' perceived lack of *any* language. We've heard other stories of overtly racist, anti-immigrant sentiment being expressed in schools. Some may remember the 2018 story of Idaho teachers dressing up as the US-Mexico border wall for Halloween or the 2024 incident in which two South Carolina teachers dressed up as Border Patrol agents during an event meant to represent "Mexican culture." Such incidents, which gained national media coverage, are extreme examples of what happens in many schools and other institutions daily. In these situations, when "good intentions" cannot be cited, there are still barriers to disrupting deficit ideologies. There may be the fear of alienation or even retaliation. There may be a sense of helplessness when such ideologies seem to be the majority opinion.

Taking Action: Off-Shoots and Leaves of Disrupting Deficit Ideologies

As critical advocates grow their awareness of deficit ideologies that shape work with MLs, they are faced with a new challenge: disrupting those ideologies in everyday discourse, local policies, pedagogical approaches, and even their relationships outside of their work. Consider the following quotes:

Voices From the Field

It's a common misunderstanding and myth among our classroom teachers that you need to speak a student's language in order to teach them. It's frustrating. It's a hard one to fight . . . like, "I don't speak Spanish, so not my problem." One of our biggest struggles is shared ownership, and we're trying to figure out [how to increase] our teachers' confidence and comfort level, especially with our newcomer students, whether they speak Spanish or Pashto or Vietnamese.

– Michelle, Multilingual Family Engagement Specialist and English Learner Instructional Coach, Wisconsin

I have a kid [who] is new, came from Mexico at the very end of last year. Brilliant child. Brilliant. But he was not getting the proper [English] instruction. So I asked the GT [Gifted and Talented] teacher, "Can we give this child the GT test, but in Spanish?" She said yes. He passed it with flying colors and qualified for GT services. If everybody would notice that we have so many brilliant kids – that sometimes the only barrier is the language, and we need to work together and bridge. We have to use the strength they have in one language to strengthen the other, because they already have such a solid foundation. That would be amazing.

– Martha, Spanish-English Dual Language teacher, Kentucky

I'm trying to be more courageous in conversations with people. For example, my mother-in-law asked me, "Do you work with illegals?" And I just kind of gently said, "We don't ask people their documentation status. At my school, we call it undocumented, we don't call it illegal. But we don't ask about that." When I hear things in conversations, instead of being worried about rocking the boat or being "that person," I'm just like, "Well, have you thought about it this way?"

– Katie, English Language Development teacher, Colorado

The lack of what Michelle called "shared ownership" can be a major barrier to disrupting deficit ideologies. The basic belief that MLs are everyone's students and that there is shared humanity across linguistic and cultural differences is integral to critical advocacy. And yet, as Michelle states, a lack of that basic belief is "a hard one to fight." But fighting that fight and disrupting deficit ideologies, even in small ways, is a highly important branch of critical advocacy.

As we can see in Martha and Katie's quotes, sometimes disruption can be the simple act of asking questions. Asking questions of practice, of assertions, of assumptions, and of policy decisions can serve as an important act of critical advocacy for MLs in schools. It is well-documented that MLs are underrepresented in Gifted and Talented and other enrichment programs (Pereira & de Oliveira, 2022). This is certainly due in large part to the deficit-oriented ideologies that frame students as incapable of participating in intellectually rigorous learning if they are not "fluent" in English. It is also due to various structural barriers; thus, the mere act of asking the question of whether the student could take a Gifted and Talented screener in his home language is an act of disruption. Martha's question – "Can we give this child the GT test, but in Spanish?" – is an enactment of her core belief in the brilliance of her students, no matter their performances in English. She envisions something better for her students, a community in which "everybody would notice that we have so many brilliant kids," and works to bring it into existence in part by asking questions that disrupt the status quo.

Asking questions and engaging in other disruptions of "common sense" discourse, teaching practices, and policies is also an act of faith in the potential of our community. Katie seems to position her disruption of her family member's deficit ideologies and lack of awareness as *teaching*. The ability to have honest, critical conversations with those we work and spend time with is an act of generosity; it is the giving of time, energy, and expertise. Katie could have simply written off her family member as a lost cause, disengaging from the conversation or lashing out in anger. Instead, she was "courageous" and asked a deceptively simple question – "Have you thought about it this way?" Such a question opens the door to new perspectives and the possibility of shifting the other party toward more awareness of and compassion for MLs.

Consider the following scenarios, which show how off-shoots and leaves of critical advocacy action can sprout from the branch of disrupting deficit ideologies:

- Concerned about the discourse she heard in her school regarding EL-designated learners and their supposed "lack of language," a family engagement coordinator asked the school principal if she could organize a shared reading and discussion of Flores's (2015) blog post, entitled "What if we talked about monolingual White children the way we talk about low-income children of color?" Though she understands that disrupting these ideas about MLs cannot happen through a one-and-done approach, she thinks the reading and discussion could be a good starting place.
- After overhearing some of her MLs joke disparagingly about each other's use of Spanish, an elementary English Language Arts teacher engaged students in a critical reading and analysis of the children's book, *Skippyjon Jones* (Schachner, 2005), to highlight the use of mock Spanish and discuss how linguistic and cultural stereotypes are perpetuated (Martínez-Roldán, 2013).
- After learning that the MLs in his classroom were feeling misunderstood by their monolingual peers, a middle school ESL teacher designed a youth participatory action research (YPAR) project that allowed students to explore and showcase aspects of their identities while also elevating their communities' and families' histories. Students' projects were then featured as part of a showcase that the entire school and community were invited to attend and remained on display during parent-teacher conferences.

Digging In: Disrupting Deficit Ideologies as Critical Advocacy

Think about how disrupting deficit ideologies would support MLs in your context. What needs have you noticed? Could you . . .

- Encourage colleagues and school leadership to refer to students as emergent multilinguals or multilingual learners rather than Limited English Proficient or English Learners?
- Design a project through which students could explore, document, and showcase their strengths and funds of knowledge with others in the school community?
- Work with counselors to identify areas where MLs are underrepresented (e.g., clubs or after-school programming, advanced or "gifted and talented" programs) and come up with strategies to diversify them?

Conclusion

Branches of critical advocacy action grow from the strong trunk of our beliefs and the deep roots of who we are. Though there are many such branches, this chapter focused on the areas of pedagogical decision-making, relationship-building and community connections, local policy-making, and disrupting deficit ideologies about MLs. We also described how off-shoots and leaves of local action can grow from these branches, benefiting MLs in schools. We hope, as you read, that you thought about the off-shoots and leaves that might grow from these branches in your own contexts. These might include asserting your teaching expertise, building bridges between your students, their families, and your colleagues, interpreting top-down policies in ways that benefit your students, or asking questions that raise awareness of and compassion for MLs in your community. These actions, big or small, have tangible effects on the lives and livelihoods of MLs, and are central to critical advocacy work.

Critical Advocacy Action Planning Connection

What can you take from this chapter's discussion of **branches, off-shoots, and leaves** into your critical advocacy action planning? You might think about how:

- **Our branches, off-shoots, and leaves are supported by a strong foundation.** Advocacy action without critical thinking and reflection can affect how meaningful, sustainable, and effective it is. It's always helpful to check in with yourself throughout the action planning process and ask: how do my roots and trunk (core beliefs) shape my approach to action? Are there advocacy actions that seem to serve MLs but don't align with my foundation?
- **Our branches, off-shoots, and leaves can grow in many directions.** All advocacy actions are shaped by who we are. Advocacy actions also come in different "sizes"; just because an action is small and hyper-local does not mean it is unimportant. To stave off the burnout and exhaustion that can accompany advocacy work, you might think about: which of the four branches of critical advocacy action do I feel most suited to? Which am I unsure of or uncomfortable with, and why? Where is a place I can "start small" with my efforts? Who can I carry out advocacy action alongside?
- **Our branches, off-shoots, and leaves grow differently in different contexts.** Not every critical advocacy action is possible in every context. Taking action must consider the specificities of your context, from the national to the state and local levels. As you engage in your

planning, you might ask: how do people in my context think about MLs? What state- or district-level policies are relevant and important to this issue? Is this action safe and viable in my context? How might perceptions of me – personally and professionally – shape my advocacy actions?

5

Preparing for the Challenges of Critical Advocacy

Anyone who has engaged in advocacy for MLs knows that it is not easy. Working against ingrained ideologies and inequitable systems is highly complex and frustrating and can take a toll on advocates' well-being. We devote a chapter of this book to the challenges of critical advocacy, not to scare you away from the work, but to help you prepare and plan for those challenges. This kind of proactive planning is not a one-time activity completed at the start of an advocacy action; it is a dynamic process that requires continuous reassessment and adjustment as new challenges and opportunities arise.

We also focus on preparing for the challenges of critical advocacy to reiterate the power and importance of the critical advocacy tree. It is in moments of deep challenge when it is most important to draw on your own histories and foundations (roots), steady yourself in your core advocacy beliefs (trunk), and view advocacy action (branches, off-shoots, and leaves) as an enactment of who you are and what you believe. We begin the chapter by exploring these potential challenges and providing some ideas to help you navigate them, including engaging in self-care practices, cultivating community, and adopting a perspective of "eyes wide open" honesty. In focusing on these self- and community-sustaining practices, we emphasize that critical advocates can face the inevitable challenges of critical

DOI: 10.4324/9781003628774-8

advocacy by caring for both their own trees and for the larger, interconnected forest they are a part of.

The Professional Challenges of Critical Advocacy

Voices From the Field

> We get pushback [about advocacy for MLs], and a lot of us are these nice, polite people. We want to be nice, and we don't want to rock the boat or be messy. So, how do you keep your job so that you can be the advocate?
>
> – Jane, Multilingual Language Learner high school English teacher, Rhode Island

Like Jane, you may have found yourself worried about the consequences of your advocacy efforts. Perhaps you engaged in a difficult conversation with a colleague that seemed to shift the tone of your relationship. Or maybe you questioned your administrator's decisions regarding placement practices for MLs and then found them to be more formal or distant with you. For many, engaging in critical advocacy for MLs places them at odds with others in their workplace because their efforts call into question administrators' and colleagues' decisions or practices. As a result, critical advocates may face professional challenges, such as resistance, pushback, and blatant opposition (i.e., rigidly enforced policies, limited resources, and increased "red tape"). These barriers make advocates' professional lives more difficult and send the message that their advocacy is unnecessary and unwelcome. Those who persist may worry, like Jane, about negative consequences such as increased surveillance and monitoring, hyper-critical evaluations, limited opportunities for professional development, and fear of demotion or job loss (Raymond et al., 2025).

Additional professional challenges can come from interpersonal conflicts. At its core, critical advocacy is about challenging and disrupting the systemic inequities and structural barriers for

MLs. Thus, those who are seen as disruptive and threatening to the status quo often make others uncomfortable and even angry. Critical advocates may experience difficult dynamics and tense relationships with colleagues who may not understand or respect the work they do. Others may find colleagues distancing themselves, pulling back on collaborations, or even excluding them from professional and social spaces. This can make critical advocacy more isolating. For many critical advocates, particularly those who work directly with students, this advocacy work occurs at the "contradictory intersection of professional responsibility and students' socio-emotional needs" (Suarez & Dominguez, 2015, p. 61). As such, by foregrounding their commitment to students, critical advocates may sacrifice their own professional relationships and socio-emotional and mental health needs.

Digging In: Exploring the Challenges of Critical Advocacy

Consider an advocacy experience you've had that you feel had a professional impact.

- How did your school community respond to your advocacy?
- Was there "fallout" from your advocacy actions, and if so, how did you navigate it?
- Were relationships broken, or was trust violated? If so, were you able to repair those relationships or move on professionally?

While professional challenges can be discouraging, it is important to recognize that there are ways to prepare for them. Consider some of the following approaches taken by critical advocates we've spoken to:

- Joining professional organizations, associations, and networks that can become additional sources of support and protection;

- Building alliances with like-minded colleagues who are in tune with your local context and can provide support;
- Creating affinity groups to share stories, strategize, and find emotional support from others in similar circumstances/with similar positionalities;
- Connecting with families and community organizations that serve MLs and can provide additional support and solidarity; and
- Engaging in professional learning opportunities that build conflict-resolution skills.

These are just a few of many ways to seek out support and allyship in the face of professional challenges related to your critical advocacy efforts.

The Personal Challenges of Critical Advocacy

Voices From the Field

I'm at that age where I'm trying to find the balance [with advocacy]. As I age, the stress that I feel when I'm advocating, I feel it in my system. There's a conflict happening, and my body feels it. And now, as I'm older, my body feels it more significantly. So I think that's a difficult side of advocacy for me.

– Stephanie, English Language Development teacher, Maryland

As Athanases and De Oliveira (2008) state, "becoming change agents can be a tall order" (p. 66). For many critical advocates like Stephanie, the inherent conflict involved in fighting deeply entrenched ideologies and norms can have a significant emotional impact and take a physical toll on advocates' health and well-being. As Chen and Gorski (2015) demonstrate, activism and social justice work can result in extreme physical and mental exhaustion, burnout, and feelings of distress, discouragement, and depression; yet many, like Stephanie, accept that the physical toll is "a difficult side of advocacy." This is particularly the case for critical advocates who may be in precarious positions due to their professional status (e.g., first-year teachers) or their own positionality (e.g., a member of a cultural or racial minority group).

Educators of color often experience what Palmer (2018) refers to as "an additional layer" of isolation and marginalization (p. 211; see also Kohli, 2018). This may be because these critical advocates are not only serving and working on behalf of minoritized communities; they are members of those communities themselves. As a result, minoritized critical advocates may experience imposter syndrome, self-doubt, and isolation as they engage in emotional labor not experienced by their white colleagues (Duncan, 2020; Rodriguez, 2024; Samuels, 2021).

The positionality of critical advocates may also play a role in how their efforts are perceived by others. The discrepancies around whose advocacy efforts are celebrated and whose are challenged or considered disruptive are immense. For example, a 2018 report from The Education Trust indicated that Latine teachers were often belittled, considered aggressive, and felt pressured to "prove their worth" by white colleagues who did not understand and/or felt threatened by these teachers' advocacy efforts (p. 2). Because of how they may find themselves labeled, critical advocates from minoritized backgrounds often have to weigh the potential consequences resulting from their silence *or* their action (Cheruvu et al., 2015; Hernández-Johnson et al., 2023).

Digging In: Knowing the Interpersonal Dynamics of Your Context

Our roots, including our identities and positionings, shape both our critical advocacy work and others' *perceptions* and *responses* to our efforts. Understanding this is an important aspect of engaging in critical advocacy with eyes wide open, which in turn can make our work more meaningful, sustainable, and effective. To grow your awareness and your ability to navigate these tensions, think about:

- How, if at all, has the nature of your advocacy differed from that of your colleagues? How might this relate to your roots?
- In the contexts in which you work, whose advocacy efforts are celebrated and whose are challenged?
- Whose advocacy efforts have been empowered and whose have been treated as acts of defiance?

Recognizing the professional and personal challenges that accompany critical advocacy is essential. It can help us prepare for the resistance we will likely encounter, the inherent power imbalances we will navigate, the emotional toll we will experience, and the risks that may accompany critical advocacy work. By acknowledging and preparing for these realities, advocates can better protect themselves and those with whom they advocate. Addressing these challenges not only sustains advocates' well-being but also strengthens their capacity to engage in advocacy work long-term. Along these lines, we next discuss strategies advocates can use to sustain their advocacy efforts.

Sustaining Our Critical Advocacy Efforts

Voices From the Field

I started off like a wrecking ball. I was in an environment where my fellow teachers were very racist, and they would say terrible things about me. And it was because I was advocating for [MLs]. So I lit the place on fire every time I saw a problem. And as I did that, I watched bridges burn. I watched teachers

> shut their doors while I walked by. I watched principals roll their eyes when they saw me come into the office. It was a very painful learning environment, but I'm glad because now I've learned that advocacy is almost a chess game. You have to know which piece to play when for the most impact. Because if you don't, you're going to get nowhere. So when I was burning bridges, I maybe could [have gotten] something in the moment, but in the long term, I didn't get anything that I needed for those kids or for myself. Now I [ask myself], is this something that needs to be addressed right now, in this moment? Or is this something I can do a little research about and come up with a more strategic way of addressing it, versus just calling people out? Because teachers and principals are vulnerable.
>
> – Jenny, English Learner Instructional Specialist, Oklahoma

For those involved in critical advocacy work, there can be "a sense of urgency and a deep emotional connection to the movements in which they engage" (Chen & Gorski, 2015, p. 20). Sometimes, that sense of urgency can mean that, like Jenny, we enter the work like a "wrecking ball," set off by an immediate need to right a wrong, but perhaps without the time to plan, or "research" a "more strategic" way of addressing the issue. The gut feeling that causes us to take action is not one we want to ignore; it is an embodied indication that something may be wrong. But rather than simply jump into action, critical advocates can tap into the elements of their tree both to guide their actions and maintain their mental and emotional well-being.

Coming to the realization that meaningful, sustainable, and effective advocacy takes time is often a difficult process and one that many, like Jenny, come to learn "the hard way." For many of us, it entails unlearning some of the problematic or deficit-oriented ideologies that have become ingrained in our perspectives and vision of advocacy. In order to ensure we have the capacity and bandwidth to handle the ups and downs of long-term critical advocacy, we must have strategies we can turn to for nourishment and recharging. We propose that by engaging in self-work and self-care, remaining grounded in community, and accepting our realities with eyes wide open, we can engage in critical advocacy while, as Mariame Kaba (2025) has put it, also fortifying ourselves for the ongoing struggle that inevitably accompanies this hard work. Doing so ensures that rather than "burning bridges" and only accomplishing "something in the moment," as Jenny described, we are engaging in advocacy efforts that are meaningful, sustainable, and effective "in the long term."

Sustaining Our Critical Advocacy Efforts Through Self-Work and Self-Care

Sustaining critical advocacy efforts requires "a deep excavation and exploration of beliefs, biases, and ideas that shape how we engage in our work" (Sealey-Ruiz, 2022, p. 22). In other words, it requires ongoing self-work, or the deep, introspective work of examining gaps in our understandings that could shape how we engage in critical advocacy (Gorski & Erakat, 2019). Self-work aligns with our core belief that perpetual learning strengthens the trunk of critical advocacy. By pausing to examine our own efforts, we may come to key realizations that allow us to fine-tune our approach. For example, like Jenny, maybe we begin to wonder about the vulnerability of those who resist our efforts or reflect on our own oversights. Feeling moved to advocate is important, but as Mentor and Sealey-Ruiz (2021) emphasize, "we have to know who we are and where we stand in order to have genuine and meaningful conversations with ourselves and others" (p. 99). This requires time, space, and ongoing commitment to increasing our self-awareness, improving our communication skills, and refining our ability to manage emotions, among other self-work skills.

While often conflated with self-work, self-care is a strategy we recommend for navigating the difficulties and exhaustion that often accompany critical advocacy work. Self-care refers to practices and strategies used by educators to reduce stress, improve overall well-being, and, ultimately, prevent burnout (Huang & Zhou, 2025). As we have emphasized, advocacy work can take a mental and emotional toll. As such, critical advocacy should include practices that help you take stock of your physical, emotional, and mental status and overall well-being. What self-care looks like or entails will vary for each person, but regardless of the form it takes, these practices should lead to increased mental and emotional clarity and, thus, greater capacity and strength to continue your advocacy efforts.

Sustaining Our Critical Advocacy Efforts Through Community

Critical advocates often experience isolation as a result of their advocacy efforts, which can add to the feelings of exhaustion and burnout that often make this work ineffective and unsustainable. It also means that advocates may operate and make decisions on their own about the needs and futures of MLs, potentially limiting the scope and intentionality of their efforts. As we discussed in Chapters 3 and 4, building community and relationships is integral to countering this isolation. When we work in community with others, we are better equipped to distribute and manage advocacy work ethically and effectively while expanding our perspectives and finding solidarity.

Voices From the Field

What I've learned over the years is you have to know what you're advocating for . . . sometimes we have these feelings of "something doesn't feel right and I'm going to advocate," but I'm not really sure what I'm advocating for other than "that's not right". So [ask yourself]: What do best practices say? What research backs it up? What data is out there? What is the policy of our district? State? What are the federal laws? You have to be aware of what all of them are.

> Because I've been with teachers who end up saying something or advocating for something that actually is bad for the program. And so this is where it's so important to have some kind of community.
>
> – Minerva, Spanish–English Dual Language teacher, Washington

Being in community, and therefore accountable not just to ourselves but others, helps us ensure that, as Minerva describes, we "know what [we are] advocating for." We take this to mean that without community – without a group of people to check in with when "something doesn't feel right" – we may end up engaging in advocacy that is counterproductive to our goals. Minerva also highlights that our community can remind us to ground our advocacy not just in feelings and instincts, but in what we know about best practice, research, data, policy, and laws. As we highlight in Chapter 3, there are many ways a community can take shape. The dialogue-oriented and supportive nature of community spaces allows critical advocates and educators to "engage the practical realities and imagined opportunities of equitable education for MLs" in ways that are in tune with the local context (Suh & Michener, 2024, p. 15). They also grant advocates necessary space to reflect on and improve their advocacy practice, build meaningful relationships with others who can support them, remain engaged with current research around best practices and approaches, and find support reflecting on ideas (Serviss, 2022).

Sustaining Our Critical Advocacy Efforts With Eyes Wide Open

As we have said throughout this book, it is essential that critical advocates enter their work with eyes wide open, meaning that they acknowledge and accept that there are things they cannot control or change. Critical advocacy, in fact, may not always be about creating *actual* change, but rather about working around the things we cannot change. For example, some of us may find ourselves in situations where we simply cannot change the larger structures shaping MLs' experiences in our schools (e.g., shifting from an English-medium program model to a bilingual model). However, that does not mean we cannot make critical changes to our own practice and classroom policies so that MLs are better supported. In this way, our advocacy efforts become not about trying to fight for changes that are very unlikely to occur but about accepting what is and is not within our control. Being eyes wide open does not mean giving up. It means being honest about the reality of the systems and structures we operate within rather than being in denial or blaming ourselves for things outside of our control.

Dubetz and de Jong (2011) called on advocates to remember that all "acts of advocacy must be considered in the context of the broader sociopolitical and professional local realities" (p. 251). We take this to mean that critical advocates must be realistic about the systems in which they operate; there will never be one single advocate or even a series of advocacy actions that can single-handedly "fix" the historically-rooted, systemic issues affecting MLs today. But critical advocacy is actually about letting go of these grandiose ideas of advocacy and resisting the idea that there is only one way to be a critical advocate.

Being eyes wide open calls on us to think about critical advocacy as a balancing act between action and rest. On one end, we remain relentless and persistent in our critical advocacy efforts, and on the other, we ensure we are caring for ourselves and each other in the process. This balancing act reminds us to move slowly because this gives us time and breathing room to be thoughtful. Instead of "[lighting] the place on fire" every time we see a problem, as Jenny put it, we can begin by acknowledging and accepting that the situation and circumstances we are encountering are not ideal, just, or acceptable. But, in order to work toward changes that are meaningful, sustainable, and effective, we have to be strategic in our next steps. What follows are a few self-work and self-care practices that cultivate an honest, eyes-wide-open mindset toward advocacy:

- **Journaling.** Consistently jot down or otherwise chronicle the feelings and thoughts you have while engaging in critical advocacy. Make space to reflect on these feelings and thoughts and note changes over time.

- **Meditation and Mindfulness.** Identify a guided meditation or mindfulness activity that speaks to you and use it as an opportunity to ground and check in with yourself.
- **Dialogue and Storytelling.** Write a dialogue or story documenting a critical advocacy experience you had; consider sharing it with others in your community as a tool for debriefing and learning together.
- **Engage in Creative "Life Writing."** Create an artistic representation (i.e., collage, video, photograph, drawing, poem) of yourself as a person, educator, and advocate. Consider representing how and why you became an educator and advocate and how your advocacy work has been impacted by "relationships, places, objects, and events in [your] life" (Shelby-Caffey et al., 2022, p. 93).

Building an honest acceptance of reality can help critical advocates remain grounded while collectively and collaboratively imagining a future that is more just and equitable for MLs. By identifying and naming the systematic and structural barriers we face while engaging in critical advocacy work alongside a practice of care for self and others, we can continue engaging in sustainable forms of advocacy that can ultimately yield long-term and far-reaching benefits.

Conclusion

Voices From the Field

This is kind of silly, but I ask myself three questions, especially when I'm spiraling, and I'm like, "I don't know if that was right." I ask myself, "Did I advocate for multilingual students and families today?" And usually the answer is yes. And then my second

> question is, "Was it awkward?" Yes. And then my third question is, "Was it worth it?" And it's always yes.
>
> – Michelle, Multilingual Learner Family Engagement Specialist and English Learner Instructional Coach, Wisconsin

Critical advocates like Michelle enter advocacy work knowing there will be challenges but also knowing that their efforts are "worth it." This chapter has explored the professional and personal challenges of critical advocacy and what it means to prepare for these challenges. We emphasize that an essential aspect of this preparation is caring for ourselves and each other. As you continue to think through your critical advocacy action planning in Part III of this book, we invite you to ask yourself a version of the questions Michelle asks herself:

- Are my advocacy efforts focused on necessary changes for ML students and families?
- Might my advocacy efforts make me or someone else feel awkward in necessary ways?
- Are my efforts worth it? And if not, what can I do differently moving forward?

By asking ourselves these questions, we enter our critical advocacy work with eyes wide open about the work, the challenges that our efforts entail, and the strength needed to persist in the struggle ahead.

Critical Advocacy Action Planning Connection

What can you take from this chapter's discussion of **challenges** into your critical advocacy action planning? You might think about how:

- **To engage in critical advocacy with eyes wide open, we must engage in self-work.** Becoming a critical advocate may require us to unlearn problematic and deficit-oriented ideologies and discourses that have become ingrained in our visions of advocacy. To continue nurturing our own growth and to assess the efficacy of our critical advocacy, we must continuously check in with ourselves. You might ask yourself: What beliefs and values shape my critical advocacy stance? Where did I learn these beliefs and values? What powers and privileges facilitate or support my ability to engage in critical advocacy efforts?

- **Critical advocacy is a balancing act: We must remain persistent in our efforts while also caring for ourselves and each other in the process.** To sustain ourselves throughout challenging seasons of advocacy, we must plan how we will care for and be accountable to ourselves and each other. You might consider asking yourself: What am I doing to process negative feelings that accompany challenges? How am I regularly taking stock of and caring for my own physical, emotional, and mental status and overall well-being?
- **For critical advocacy to be sustainable, we must intentionally cultivate and remain grounded in community.** In order for our efforts to be meaningful, sustainable, and effective, we cannot operate in isolation. When we work in community with others, we build relational systems of accountability that support and facilitate our own growth and development and ensure that our efforts are sustainable. As you consider your own community, you may ask yourself: Who do I work alongside? How do these relationships sustain me and my efforts? How might I continue to cultivate and build community?

Part III

Growing Meaningful, Sustainable, and Effective Critical Advocacy Action

Parts I and II of this book explored critical advocacy through the extended metaphor of the critical advocacy tree. Part I walked you through a critical examination of your own roots – those you forged in your early years, those you've extended over time through personal and professional experiences, and those that are bound up in the deficit-oriented ideologies that have shaped the ways MLs are educated in schools and treated in society. It also helped you delve into your trunk, the core beliefs that inform your critical advocacy.

Part II explored how critical advocacy action – the branches and off-shoots that extend and sprout from our tree – is an enactment of your core beliefs and helps make critical advocacy for MLs a reality. We discussed areas of critical advocacy actions that relate to pedagogy, community-building, local policy-making, and disrupting deficit ideologies, and we offered ideas for how critical advocates can sustain themselves and those around them throughout their actions. We emphasized that by being honest about the challenges of critical advocacy and planning for ways to navigate those challenges thoughtfully, critical advocates can avoid burnout and persist in their efforts.

In this third and final section of our book, we invite you to think more about off-shoots and leaves, or local critical advocacy action. Chapter 6 introduces you to scenarios that explore complex situations faced by critical advocates for MLs. As you read through what the critical advocates in these scenarios face – from instructional and programmatic decision-making to managing interpersonal conflicts to navigating racist, xenophobic ideologies – you will also consider critical questions that we hope will deepen your own approach to critical advocacy for MLs.

DOI: 10.4324/9781003628774-9

Chapter 7 presents the Critical Advocacy Action Planning Tool, which can help you plan your own meaningful, effective, and sustainable critical advocacy action. As we go through each element of this tool, we'll call back to ideas you've already been introduced to that relate those elements to our critical advocacy tree. You will also find examples of critical advocacy action planning that show how two critical advocates engaged with the tool. It is our hope that using this Critical Advocacy Action Planning Tool will help you not only develop ideas and strategies for working toward educational equity for MLs, but also a framework for doing so in ways that are responsive to your local needs and context.

We end the book with a conclusion that aims both to summarize our ideas and offer seeds of wisdom for those who wish to step into critical advocacy work. These seeds of wisdom, drawn from critical advocates who have been through many seasons of personal and professional growth, emphasize the importance of honesty and hope when working toward equity for MLs in schools.

6

Connecting the Every-Day to Critical Advocacy Action

Throughout the book, we have drawn on our metaphor of the critical advocacy tree to explore how enactments of critical advocacy – the off-shoots and leaves of our efforts – are firmly rooted, strengthened, and supported by who we are (our roots), what we believe (our trunk), and the core actions we take (our branches, off-shoots, and leaves). This version of advocacy goes beyond just "taking action"; it embraces the criticality and thoughtfulness we believe is necessary to meaningful, sustainable, and effective advocacy. To help demonstrate this kind of advocacy and to get you thinking about your own, this chapter invites you to engage with scenarios that illustrate how:

- ♦ Opportunities for critical advocacy exist in the everyday work of educators who support MLs;
- ♦ Critical advocacy can align with our roles, strengths, and passions; and
- ♦ Every critical advocacy effort requires thoughtfulness about ourselves (the personal), our broader contexts (the political), and our work in schools (the pedagogical).

These scenarios are composites, created from the stories we've heard in our conversations with critical advocates. Like many real-life situations you have no doubt faced, these scenarios

DOI: 10.4324/9781003628774-10

resist easy interpretation and answers; they require the kind of analysis and thinking that is integral to critical advocacy. For this reason, in addition to laying out the four scenarios and providing analysis of each one, we pose questions that invite you to think beyond simple "solutions" to the perceived problem(s). This chapter is not only an opportunity to think through timely, real-world critical advocacy scenarios; it sets the stage for the critical advocacy action planning you will do in the final chapter of the book.

Scenario 1: Connecting Instructional Expertise to Critical Advocacy Action

Matthew is an Instructional Specialist at a high school that has seen an influx of unaccompanied minors. Like unaccompanied minors across the country, most of these students are male and have traveled from Central and South America. Most, but not all, speak Spanish, and many also speak Indigenous languages. In his work with these students, Matthew has found that many have experienced trauma and nearly all of them have had inconsistent schooling in their home countries. However, Matthew has also found that these students are highly independent, resourceful, and eager to learn. Once an ESL teacher, Matthew's work is now focused on working with teachers across content areas to develop their understandings of what these students have faced and to hone asset-based, trauma-informed approaches so they can leverage the strengths these students bring.

There is a big debate among the small team of administrators at Matthew's school about what program model would best serve these students. Some advocate for creating a special "newcomer" program and placing all unaccompanied minors there for at least a few months. Those who support this plan say that a newcomer program would help acclimate students, both to English and to the US school system. Such a program would also help meet some of these students' unique social-emotional needs. Other administrators on the team believe that programming these students into "mainstream," general education classrooms is the way to go. They argue that students need an inclusive, supportive approach that positions them as members of the community from the start and integrates them socially, academically, and linguistically.

In his role as an Instructional Specialist, Matthew is often positioned between administrators and teachers, helping inform institutional decision-making and priorities and "translating" those into instructional practice. As the debate over how to work with these unaccompanied minors persists, he's been asked to help the administrative team figure out the best course of action for programming and teaching these newly arrived MLs. As he thinks through this programmatic and pedagogical decision, he also taps into his strong sense of responsibility to help teachers serve *all* students. This, he believes, must include both pedagogical approaches and a focus on the deficit discourse he's heard circulating (i.e., "they don't have *any* language" or "these kids have been through so much, school is the least of their problems"). Matthew has a meeting with the administrative team next week to give his recommendations.

Analysis and Questions to Consider for Critical Advocacy Action

Like many educators across the country, Matthew and his administrative team are faced with serving a population of students that has great, and highly varied, needs. Serving unaccompanied minors requires not just a sound instructional plan (i.e., how to meet students' academic and linguistic needs) but flexibility around programming, the ability to navigate cultural differences, and trauma-informed approaches that consider students' mental and physical health (Evans et al., 2022). Schools are often unprepared to meet the needs of these students, lacking both the capacity and knowledge to educate them. Thankfully, in Matthew's school, his administrative team is being thoughtful about how to work with unaccompanied minors; they are willing to think creatively, they have students' best interests in mind, and they are seeking out someone like Matthew with the instructional expertise to help them reach the best possible solution.

As Matthew considers the recommendations he'll give to his administration, he will most certainly draw on his strong, career-long commitment both to teachers and ML students. That commitment is not just to teach ML students well; it's to work with their teachers to confront the deficit ideologies about these students that circulate through schools. As such, part of what Matthew will consider is the stigma that unaccompanied minors carry with them into US schools and how that shapes teachers' perceptions of them as learners. From Matthew's roots as an ESL teacher, he knows how such a stigma can affect more than just perceptions; it can actually shape how MLs are taught and treated in schools (Dabach, 2014). Central to his work and advocacy are empathy and compassion, the core belief that all ML students, especially those who have been through what unaccompanied minors have, deserve teachers who know how to teach them.

Matthew will also have to consider the programming options his administration is debating. In his graduate work, Matthew learned about different program models and the benefits and drawbacks of each. He knows that while newcomer programs can serve as safe havens for students that help them acclimate to the academic, cultural, and linguistic expectations of US schools, they are highly complex to organize (Wright, 2025). Would his administration have the capacity to develop this kind of program thoughtfully so that students would be truly supported? On the other hand, "mainstreaming" these students might put a lot of pressure on teachers, who Matthew knows already have so much on their plates. Matthew also wonders about the legality of such a decision, given what he recalls about the *Lau v. Nichols* 1974 case, which ruled that public schools must provide accommodations and language services to ensure EL-designated students have opportunities for meaningful participation and learning. Without PD, resources, and the time and space to learn about how to meet these students' unique academic (and other) needs, teachers may feel overwhelmed and under-supported, and his school may be out of compliance.

Because of Matthew's role as an Instructional Specialist and his expertise in teaching MLs from his previous career as an ESL teacher, he is well-positioned to focus on the branches of pedagogical decision-making and local policy-making to take action on this issue. However, before he dives into any critical advocacy action, there are some questions he might want to ask himself:

- Do I know enough about this particular population of students? Have I educated myself through research that includes implications for schools and teachers?
- Do I know of any person or organization outside of the school who works with unaccompanied minors and might lend insight into this programming question?
- How can I ensure that my pedagogical decision-making is meaningfully grounded in the needs and interests of this group of MLs?

Digging In: Reflecting on Matthew's Scenario

If Matthew were your colleague, how might you help him come up with recommendations for his administration? What might he be missing that your positioning, experience, and expertise allow you to see and understand? Do you have any knowledge that would help him answer the preceding questions?

Scenario 2: Connecting Empathy and Relationship-Building to Critical Advocacy Action

Julia, a Parent Coordinator, is struggling to work with a family in her school community. The elementary school where she works has received a number of Ukrainian families who have fled the ongoing Russian invasion of their home country. Julia is the child of refugee parents herself, a part of her identity that drew her to work with MLs and their families. Though her school is generally supportive of recently arrived students, Julia finds that she is often advocating not just for things like interpreters and other family services but for her colleagues and administrators to see these students as the same as their English-speaking, American-born peers. It can be frustrating, but Julia has found that most members of her community want to learn and be more accepting of ML students and families. Despite this potential openness and empathy, Julia has noticed that there isn't a lot of training about how to serve MLs. Though she's not a teacher, she has heard from teacher colleagues that most of their professional development time is spent on other initiatives, such as the Science of Reading, without attention paid specifically to MLs.

The family Julia is working with is having a hard time getting their 10-year-old daughter situated in the school. After initially assessing the child, the school wanted to place her in a second-grade classroom due to her lack of English and the interrupted schooling she experienced over the past few years in Ukraine. Her parents contested this decision; they said their daughter had completed fourth grade in Ukraine prior to the start of the invasion, though they did not have the documentation to show it. As a result of the family's advocacy and Julia's empathy and ability to liaise between them and the school, the child was placed in a mainstream fifth-grade classroom. The family appreciated this, but has begun to fear that their daughter is unable to keep up. Though she receives pull-out English language services with an ESL teacher, there is little support or scaffolding in her English-medium general education classroom. The parents are very concerned and feel misunderstood and unsupported. They have asked Julia for guidance on how to move forward.

Analysis and Questions to Consider for Critical Advocacy Action

As a Parent Coordinator and a child of refugee parents herself, Julia knows too well how opaque the school system can be for immigrant families, particularly those who have experienced hardship. Though it is well-documented that families of MLs care deeply about their children's education (Maldonado Torres, 2022; Song, 2023), it can be difficult for them to navigate the specific (and often unwritten) norms, rules, and expectations set by schools. For example, though the family insisted that their daughter completed fourth grade in Ukraine, they did not have the documentation necessary to show it. The family may not have known this would be necessary, or did not have the time or ability to secure this documentation amidst the conflict in their home country. It is also possible that their school in Ukraine did not organize their documentation in this manner, leaving the family unable to support their case for placing their child in her appropriate grade level.

Another challenge Julia faces is the overall lack of understanding of MLs and their families. Though she has found her community open and accepting of MLs, she often carries the burden of educating her colleagues about these students. There is little institutional support or professional development that could amplify Julia's messaging and help inform her colleagues of not only the difficulties these families face, but also the rich affordances they bring. This lack of awareness is evident in the school's initial placement decision. Though the assessments the school used pointed to the child's lack of English proficiency and grade-level content knowledge, research has shown that such assessments often miss what MLs know and can do (Ascenzi-Moreno, 2018; Wang & Li, 2020). Rather than place the child in a learning environment that is developmentally and age-appropriate for her (with necessary supports), the school let monolingual, standardized assessments guide the placement process.

Julia's critical advocacy is closely tied to her roots, namely her identity as the child of refugee parents. This background is at the heart of her work with MLs and is the main source of both her empathy and her drive to serve these students and their families well. Her own experiences as the child of immigrants have also imbued her with the core belief that families are essential partners in educating their children. She does not shoehorn immigrant children and families into US schooling; she sees herself as a perpetual learner, getting to know their experiences and aspirations so she can serve them well.

In this scenario, Julia's commitment to building relationships with families and advocating for their needs has led these Ukrainian parents to see her as a trusted ally. They rely on her to facilitate communication with the school, represent and promote their position, and ideally get them the outcome they desire: a supportive, accessible, age-appropriate classroom placement.

Thus, Julia must think through which branch of critical advocacy is best suited to the case and would result in the most meaningful, sustainable, and effective action. Because of her role as a Parent Coordinator and because of her own identity, she sees relationship-building and community connections as her strength and expertise. Some questions Julia might ask herself as she charts her course of action are:

- What relationships can I leverage and/or further develop to address this situation?
- Who would need to be included and what would need to be done to ensure that my efforts are sustainable (i.e., not a one-off fix, but a system-focused, collaborative approach)?
- What consequences, roadblocks, or setbacks might I face in carrying out this action, and how will I navigate them?

Digging In: Reflecting on Julia's Scenario

If Julia were your colleague, how might you help her advocate for this family? What other branches of critical advocacy could you suggest that would deepen the impact on this one family's situation? Do you have any knowledge, experiences, or insights that would help her answer the preceding questions?

Scenario 3: Connecting Interpersonal Conflicts to Critical Advocacy Action

Mina is a district administrator in charge of World Languages and English as a Second Language programs. In addition to training teachers of MLs in research-based instructional approaches, Mina is passionate about ensuring that her district is in compliance with all federal, state, and local laws and that MLs and their families know their rights. As a strong advocate and a Farsi-English bilingual herself, when MLs' rights to an equitable education and schooling experience are challenged, Mina is not afraid to speak out. This has, at times, led to tensions between Mina and her colleagues, but her candor, compassion, and ability to navigate difficult conversations have made her a well-respected leader. Though Mina works in a very liberal state, her district is more conservative, and it is not uncommon to hear racist, xenophobic rhetoric about MLs. It is also not uncommon for such ideologies to manifest more implicitly, through microaggressions and low expectations of students.

At this year's Back to School Night, Mina made sure that every single family of MLs in attendance was assigned their own interpreter who accompanied them throughout the evening, helping them understand what the administrators, teachers, and other staff told them. The day after the event, a teacher angrily approached Mina in the hallway. The young math teacher, who had only started at the school a few months ago, told her that he was distracted by the interpreters who assisted at Back to School Night. Mina first asked a few questions: "What about their presence distracted you? Did you think they weren't translating what you were saying?" Despite his anger, the teacher could not articulate exactly why the interpreters had distracted him and thrown him "off his game." When Mina probed further, the teacher told her that he did not like how the parents were looking at the interpreters, not at him, when he spoke to them. He also thought the parents were "making faces" at the interpreters when he spoke, which he felt was disrespectful. When Mina tried to ask more questions, the teacher told her he didn't want to talk about it anymore and stormed off. Mina must now figure out how she will respond.

Analysis and Questions to Consider for Critical Advocacy Action

Though Mina is not afraid to speak her mind, she is faced with a complex situation. She is fairly certain that this young teacher's anger is a projection of his own anxiety and discomfort related to Back to School Night. Though she was not present for this teacher's parent meetings, she imagines him feeling shut out from what the families of his students were saying, questioning the interpreter's accuracy, and wishing these kinds of interactions were simply *easier.* Though it would be understandable for Mina's own emotions to arise – anger at this teacher's lack of professionalism, frustration at the interpersonal barriers to fulfilling parents' legal rights – she is a leader and wants to approach this situation as a teachable moment.

One of the things Mina considers is her positionality vis-à-vis the teacher's. She is a woman of color, and though she was born in the US, she shares the bilingual/bicultural experiences of many of the district's ML students. The teacher is male, white, and monolingual English-speaking, likely lacking some of the connections that Mina has with students and families. Though Mina does not supervise this teacher, there is also a power imbalance at play; he is a new teacher, and she is a seasoned professional in a leadership role. Additionally, because of Mina's administrative position, she is privy to the bigger picture regarding events like Back to School Night. The teacher's role is to communicate with families about how their children are doing in his math class. Mina has much less "face time" with individual families at such events and is more concerned with their overall access. All of these elements affect Mina's point of view and play a role in how she will approach the situation.

Despite the importance of understanding where this teacher is coming from, Mina is also a staunch advocate for MLs and their rights. As someone new to the profession, it's important that this teacher learn that providing these parents with interpreters does more than create a welcoming environment; it ensures that schools in the district are in compliance with the legal rights of MLs. In addition, if left unaddressed, this teacher might take his (unfounded) anger and resentment into future interactions with students and their families, which is unacceptable. Though Mina wants to approach the conversation with the teacher from a place of compassion, she also wants to make it exceedingly clear that his behavior was not ok and that his students and their families received – and will continue to receive – the services they both deserve and are legally entitled to.

Mina's strengths – honesty, directness, and a passion for ensuring an equitable education for MLs – and her professional expertise equip her to address this situation meaningfully. And though this is an interpersonal conflict, Mina knows it is potentially representative of something bigger – broader deficit-oriented ideologies among teachers, an overall lack of awareness and understanding of MLs' rights, or a sense of unpreparedness to navigate having MLs in the classroom among newer faculty. Some questions Mina might ask herself as she considers her next move include:

- How can I address this teacher's behavior honestly and also focus on his growth and learning?
- What risks might I face in this conversation, and how can I prepare for them?
- How can I draw on this individual situation to make my efforts broader and more sustainable (i.e., to spark a wider shift in culture, attitudes, or training around MLs)?

Digging In: Reflecting on Mina's Scenario

If Mina were your colleague, how might you help her both to navigate this interpersonal conflict *and* think beyond it? What other branches of critical advocacy could you suggest that would deepen the impact of this individual conversation? Do you have any information, experiences, or insights that would help her answer the preceding questions?

Scenario 4: Connecting Ideological Resilience to Critical Advocacy Action

Ana is an ESL teacher who works closely with ML students across several schools in a small, rural district. Despite the proportionally large number of MLs in the district, the majority of the community is still made up of white, working-class families. Though there has been some tension between those families and the immigrant community, the administrators and teachers in Ana's district have done a great job making the schools accessible, welcoming, and engaging for MLs. Due in large part to Ana and her fellow teachers' leadership, there are strong policies and systems in place for assessing and placing students, providing English language services, and meaningfully integrating ML students with their English-speaking peers.

Ana and a small group of her colleagues, most of whom, including Ana, are Spanish-English bilingual Latine women, have lived and worked in the community for many years and are highly respected. They are also very close and have bonded over their shared passion for teaching MLs. They have even shared that passion with their school community, providing other teachers in the district with PD on topics ranging from the use of students' home languages to scaffolding and differentiating instruction for MLs at different levels of English proficiency. The work hasn't been easy, but Ana and her colleagues have helped the district become known within the state for serving MLs well.

In March 2025, President Trump signed Executive Order 14224, which designated English as the official language of the United States. Despite other federal and state laws that prohibit discrimination against people with limited English proficiency, the Executive Order sent shock waves through Ana's small, close-knit community. Soon after it was signed, several members of the majority white, English-speaking community attended the district's monthly School Board meeting and demanded that the schools teach "English only" and eliminate their "DEI" work. After the meeting, the Superintendent calls all district principals together to discuss how they will respond to the Executive Order and the community's push-back. In response, the principal of one of the schools Ana works in calls a meeting for all ESL teachers and ML specialists to discuss next steps. Ana can tell the principal is nervous and is looking to her and her colleagues to help him move forward.

Analysis and Questions to Consider for Critical Advocacy Action

Those like Ana and her colleagues who have worked with MLs for a long time know that the socio-political forces that swing the proverbial pendulum either toward or away from equitable schooling for MLs deeply affect their day-to-day work. Though their beliefs and advocacy efforts do not necessarily change, they must evolve and adapt to meet the moment. This is a delicate balance, one that all critical advocates must navigate: staying true to one's own core beliefs while also choosing tactics that enable them to persist in the work. As we discussed in Chapter 5, Mariame Kaba's (2025) helpful booklet on making a plan for activism and community organizing includes an important prompt: "How will you fortify yourself for the ongoing struggle?" (p. 6). Ana and her colleagues, like generations of critical advocates who came before them, must consider this question as they take on this new wave of anti-immigrant, anti-bilingual backlash.

One of the ways they can fortify themselves is by expanding the community they have already forged. As we discussed in Chapter 5, community can be an antidote to burnout, allowing advocates to find solidarity, "pass the baton" when necessary, and broaden their perspectives and the scope of their work. Though Ana and her colleagues will most certainly counter the English-only and anti-DEI rhetoric with professional expertise, research, and local data that demonstrates the success of their efforts with MLs in the district, they must also draw from and continually replenish the deep well of their collective resilience, passion, and energy. Ana and her colleagues have already accompanied one another on the journey of reforming their teaching and their schools by questioning deficit-oriented beliefs and pedagogical practices that do not recognize the potential of MLs. As they take on yet another iteration of this work, they can lean on one another *and* seek out new allies in the struggle, expanding their circle to include more like-minded people.

Another benefit of community, and particularly a diverse one, is that it can insulate people like Ana and her bilingual, Latine colleagues from the outsize consequences people of color experience in educational advocacy work (Gorski & Erakat, 2019). Though their positioning has enabled Ana and her colleagues to strengthen their schools' approaches to working with MLs, it may also place a target on their backs in a community that has been emboldened to voice its racism and xenophobia. Ana and her fellow teachers are no doubt aware of this reality and of the ways that raciolinguistic ideologies (Flores & Rosa, 2015) negatively affect how they are perceived. By strengthening their relationships and inviting others, including their principal, to join them in critiquing the harmful ideologies that fuel the current backlash, Ana and her colleagues can be more effective and *safer* in their critical advocacy efforts.

As Ana and her colleagues fortify themselves for the ongoing struggle, they might consider the following questions:

- What elements of our identities and beliefs can we tap into when critical advocacy work feels very heavy?
- How can we create protected time and space not only to strategize pedagogically and politically, but to support one another personally?
- Who else can we bring into this work that will strengthen our collective critical advocacy efforts?

Digging In: Reflecting on Ana's Scenario

If you worked with Ana and her colleagues, how would you help them take on this ideological and pedagogical challenge? What branches of advocacy would you suggest? Do you have any information, experiences, or insights that would help her answer the preceding questions?

Conclusion

This chapter introduced you to four scenarios that would benefit from thoughtful, critical advocacy action. The situations that Matthew, Julia, Mina, and Ana must confront require self-reflection, commitment to their asset-oriented beliefs about MLs and core beliefs about advocacy, critical thinking about what actions align with both the problem and their own roles and strengths, and their responsibility to center the needs and aspirations of the MLs they work with. Perhaps, as you were reading, you found yourself thinking about times when you've faced a dilemma or had to engage in high-stakes decision-making that affected the education of MLs. Hopefully, the analysis we offered and the questions we posed not only helped you to engage with the scenarios but also to think about your own. We also hope that these scenarios demonstrate that the off-shoots and leaves of critical advocacy are not always big, bold action. There are opportunities for critical advocacy in your everyday work with MLs, and that advocacy can and *should* align with your existing roles, strengths, and passions. When we think of critical advocacy not as something "extra" but as a consistent process of being thoughtful about ourselves (the personal), our broader contexts (the political), and our school-based work (the pedagogical), our efforts become more meaningful, sustainable, and effective.

Critical Advocacy Action Planning Connection

This chapter explored four scenarios that require critical advocacy action planning. We offered an analysis of what the critical advocates featured in each scenario might consider, as well as questions for you to think about in terms of "next steps." We hope this chapter helps you think about these additional questions, which are central to our Critical Advocacy Action Planning Tool. You can think about them in terms of the scenarios you encountered in this chapter, or you can think about them generally in regard to your own context:

- ♦ How are aspects of my roots/identity potentially shaping my interpretations and efforts?
- ♦ Who am I involving in my advocacy efforts, and who might be missing?
- ♦ How am I incorporating the needs/perspectives of those I am trying to advocate for into my efforts?

- What consequences, roadblocks, or setbacks might I face in carrying out my efforts, and how will I contend with them?
- How will I "fortify myself for the on-going struggle" (Kaba, 2025) that accompanies critical advocacy?

7

Putting It All Together

The Critical Advocacy Action Planning Tool

Across this book, you have reflected on your own identity, considered your stance and beliefs, and unpacked what motivates and grounds you in your critical advocacy efforts. This chapter is a culmination of that work and invites you to plan for critical advocacy action in your own context through the use of the Critical Advocacy Action Planning Tool (see Appendix A for a copy of the tool in full). To show how the tool can work in action, we feature the critical advocacy action planning of two critical advocates: Michelle from Wisconsin and Dr. Dilini from New York.

We recognize that the level of detail, reflection, and planning seen in their work may not always be possible; however, we hope that some of the reflection we discuss here will, over time and with practice, become an inherent part of how you approach your advocacy efforts. We encourage you to think of the questions included in the tool not as an exhaustive list that must be worked through in full, but rather as a set of guidelines and opportunities to pause and reflect on your critical advocacy planning process.

Ideally, you will use the Critical Advocacy Action Planning Tool in community with others, discussing similarities, differences, and emerging themes in how you approach and engage in critical advocacy work. With that said, we also recognize that you may

DOI: 10.4324/9781003628774-11

feel like the "sole" advocate for MLs in your specific context. For those of you who find yourself in this position, we hope that the planning tool will serve as a resource for identifying potential points of connection and collaboration.

In the sections that follow, we describe the process of:

1. Identifying an issue related to MLs in your local context;
2. Brainstorming how to address the issue;
3. Articulating a goal you hope to accomplish;
4. Considering the goal in your local context; and
5. Critically assessing and reflecting on your progress.

For each stage of this tool, we also include questions for reflection and connections to other parts of the book that will help you ensure that your actions are meaningful, sustainable, and effective. This planning process emphasizes that advocacy is as much about listening, learning, and recalibrating as it is about action. Approaching critical advocacy in this way also allows us to engage with eyes wide open, attentive to how our stances and beliefs shape who we involve, whose perspectives are centered, what consequences may arise, and how we respond to them, and how we care for ourselves and one another.

Identify an Issue, Opportunity, or Area of Concern That Relates to MLs in Your Context

As you've read this book, you've likely thought about questions or concerns you have about how MLs experience school in your community. The very first stage of critical advocacy action planning is to narrow your focus and identify one of those questions, concerns, or opportunities to address. This initial act of identifying a route for critical advocacy action may seem simple, but if we want that action to be *critical*, the internal, self-work we've discussed throughout this book is a necessary first step.

In Chapters 1 and 2, we asked you to think about your roots and how they shape what you care about and what you perceive to be just or unjust. You thought about how your roots have grown and continue to expand through your personal and professional experiences. You also thought about the ideologies that have shaped your roots and influenced how you think about MLs and concepts like language, bilingualism, immigration, race, culture, and ability. Your roots are the foundation of all critical advocacy action and must therefore be considered honestly at all stages of the planning process. As you identify the issue you'd like to take action on, we encourage you to ask yourself:

- How are aspects of my roots/identity potentially shaping my interpretations and efforts?
- Why does this issue matter to me?
- How did I come to learn about this issue? Who raised it?
- What assumptions am I making about this issue?

Engaging meaningfully with these questions will not only help you better understand your own critical advocacy action; it will enable you to engage in self-work that sheds light on your existing beliefs and potential gaps in understanding. For this reason, as always, we encourage you to collaborate with others in your community to dialogue about these questions. What might come up in initial conversations about the issue you identify? What new perspectives might emerge as you voice your questions and concerns with others? How might the action plan you initiate become more nuanced and meaningful as you share it with critical friends?

As you engage in this early stage of critical advocacy action planning, you can return to Chapter 1's *Digging In: Exploring Your Roots* activity that asks a series of questions about how your roots relate to your identity and understanding of what MLs experience in school. You can also revisit the deficit-oriented ideologies we explored in Chapter 2 and reflect critically on how those may influence your identification of an issue *and* your initial instincts regarding action planning. Reminding yourself of some of the well-intentioned, but ultimately problematic, framings of advocacy (i.e., the pobrecito syndrome) could help ground your efforts in more ethical ways of taking action.

Critical advocate Dr. Dilini, an English as a New Language teacher from New York, describes what drives her desire to work on behalf of MLs who are also identified as students with disabilities. She engaged with the question of how she landed on the (mis)identification of this sub-population of MLs as an issue she wanted to address:

Voices From the Field

In my context, I've seen far too often how MLs are either over-identified for special education due to limited English proficiency being misinterpreted as a disability, or under-identified because educators assume language is the only barrier. This matters to me not only as an educator and leader but also as a former ELL myself, who knows how easy it is to be misunderstood in a system that isn't always equipped to see students' full potential through a culturally and linguistically responsive lens. . . . This issue is not just professional for me – it's personal. I see myself in my students. I see their strengths being overlooked. And I feel a responsibility to advocate for better systems that honor both their language and their learning needs without forcing them to choose between the two.

Here, Dr. Dilini reflects honestly on why the issue of identification of dually-identified students is of such deep concern to her. She writes that the issue is personal because she sees herself, a former ML from Sri Lanka, in her students. The idea that their strengths, like her own, may be overlooked because their language and learning needs are not being met is an issue Dr. Dilini clearly feels strongly about addressing. As she thinks through her identification of this issue and how she wants to address it, its personal nature to her is something she might continue to reflect on. She might think about what her strong sense of empathy and compassion for her students – a core critical advocacy belief – enables her to see and understand in terms of (in)justice. She might also think about how her own lens could be widened through additional learning and collaboration with others who offer new perspectives on the issue.

Brainstorm How You Can Address This Issue, Opportunity, or Concern

Once you have identified an issue, question, or opportunity, it is time to think about how you will address it through critical advocacy action. There are several considerations in this stage of planning. First, you can reflect on *yourself* as a critical advocate, asking yourself:

- ◆ What are my strengths and how can I use them in my advocacy efforts?
- ◆ What sorts of advocacy actions am I comfortable with and well-suited to taking part in?

As we discussed in Chapter 4, there is no one way to engage in critical advocacy. Despite the common framing of advocacy as outsized, heroic efforts that change the course of history, we think of critical advocacy action as *any* enactment of your beliefs that positively shapes the experiences of MLs and contributes to educational equity. To ensure that your efforts are sustainable, you can think about what you *already* bring to the table: what you're good at, what you enjoy doing, what connections and relationships you already have, and what kinds of advocacy actions you find yourself drawn to.

Next, you can think about which branches of advocacy action organically lend themselves to the question you're asking or issue you're raising. In Chapter 4, we described four branches: pedagogical decision-making, relationship/community-building, local policy-making, and challenging deficit ideologies and discussed how local actions – off-shoots and leaves – can sprout from them and lead to meaningful shifts in how we educate and serve MLs. As you think about your own off-shoots and leaves, it may be helpful to ask yourself:

- ◆ What branches of action (pedagogical decision-making, relationship/community-building, local policy-making, and/or challenging deficit ideologies) lend themselves to this issue?

Lastly, because collaboration and perpetual learning are two of the core beliefs that ensure that the trunk of your critical advocacy tree is strong and sturdy, it is important to brainstorm ways that you can widen your lens and seek out additional and alternative perspectives. You can look back at Chapter 3's *Digging In: Resources for Community Building* and ask yourself:

- What collaborations can I seek out or strengthen to address this issue?
- What additional learning opportunities are there for me to understand this issue?

Asking yourself these questions ensures you are actively planning for the kind of expansive and relational advocacy we see as essential when working with MLs. Particularly for those of us whose roots grew outside of the communities we now wish to advocate alongside, we must understand that we do not know what we do not know. You might think about:

- Who am I involving in these efforts, and who might be missing?
- How am I incorporating the needs/perspectives of those I am trying to advocate for into this goal?

You should not see your own gaps in understanding as points of shame or guilt. Acknowledging these gaps and meaningfully connecting yourself with people, resources, and information that can supplement and expand your view is what makes you a *critical* advocate.

Voices From the Field

Michelle, a Multilingual Family Engagement Specialist and English Learner Instructional Coach from Wisconsin, saw that her school struggled to communicate with families of MLs who speak languages other than English. Because of her strong belief in the importance of communication to both student success and family empowerment, she brainstormed how to address this issue. Because her professional role already included an emphasis on relationship-building within and beyond the school, Michelle focused on that branch of action for developing responsive, multilingual communication efforts. One of the things she included in this brainstorming stage was creating a needs assessment that would help her better understand the issue from a variety of perspectives. Michelle thought about who should be involved, from ML families and teachers to nurses, front office staff, and any family-facing members of the community. Drawing on that needs assessment, Michelle brainstormed ways of using her strengths and existing role to build the relationships that would improve communication efforts, such as developing a clear process whereby different members of the school community could report and speak to her about a family communication need.

As you can see from our narration of Michelle's planning, she used this stage to think through both what she knew and what she *wanted* to know about the issue of communication with families of MLs. Leveraging her personal strengths and professional expertise in relationship-building, Michelle considered who might help her flesh out her understanding of this issue, including people like nurses and front office staff who are not typically involved in these processes. Starting with a "needs assessment" was one way she could both learn from and deepen her relationships with these colleagues. She also identified relationship-building as a possible branch of action for addressing this issue, brainstorming a process by which *anyone* who worked at the school, not just teachers of MLs, could contribute to improving communication with families. Such a system would be a meaningful, sustainable, and effective way for Michelle to enact positive change.

Consider the Issue in Terms of Your Local Context

Increasingly, educators find themselves at the center of political debates and culture wars in schools and classrooms. For this reason, we have emphasized the importance of familiarizing yourself with the specific dynamics of your own context. For example, as teacher educators working in the state of New Jersey, we know that how we talk about MLs and the programming options afforded to them is more open and pro-bilingual than in other states. Thus, while advocates have always been savvy about their advocacy for MLs, the rising xenophobic and English-only sentiments and policies in many states and districts have made this work more precarious. As you explore the critical advocacy action you will take, we encourage you to ask yourself:

- What are local perspectives on MLs? How will I account for and address these perspectives?

At the same time, understanding who *you* are and how your work and role are perceived by others is essential to navigating local contexts. You can ask yourself:

- How am I viewed personally and professionally in my context? Will others' perceptions of me help or hinder my actions?
- Have I learned enough about who is already doing this work and/or what resources already exist?
- What consequences, roadblocks, or setbacks might I face in carrying out this action, and how will I contend with them?

As we discussed in Chapter 5, we know that advocates face different challenges based on their identities and positionalities. In reflecting on these questions, we encourage critical advocates to take responsibility for themselves and their own actions while also recognizing the impact of others' *perceptions of* and *responses to* their efforts. By tapping into external resources and support systems, critical advocates can plug into structures that will not only protect and support them and their work but also hold them accountable to themselves and to the MLs they serve.

In preparation for designing a critical advocacy action plan, Dr. Dilini reflected on her local context, recognizing how both MLs and she herself were positioned in her setting:

Voices From the Field

While there is growing awareness of the importance of linguistic diversity and cultural responsiveness, I still see traces of deficit thinking, particularly when students don't meet benchmarks at the same pace as their monolingual peers. In some cases, well-intentioned educators express concern in ways that reflect limited understanding of the language acquisition process. . . . When I first started teaching, I was very uncomfortable in my building because I was the only person who was not white. And I had to get used to that. I think it's different when I'm the one who's advocating, and I'm the one who looks like this.

In Chapter 2's *Digging In: Adopting a Critical, Assets-oriented Lens* about the deficit-oriented perspectives that permeate school contexts, you may have documented barriers to your critical advocacy work that are rooted in your community's lack of familiarity with and understanding of MLs. Like Dr. Dilini, you will have to account for and name these perspectives in order to adequately address them.

In Chapter 5's *Digging In: Knowing the Interpersonal Dynamics of your Context* about difficult critical advocacy experiences, we discussed how understanding and accounting for the challenges you will face as an advocate is essential for engaging in critical advocacy with eyes wide open. Doing so is also necessary for ensuring your students' and your own safety. To that end, we encourage you to *always* ask yourself:

- Is the way I want to address this issue actually viable and safe in my context?

In the case of Dr. Dilini, before she can confront the deficit-oriented perspectives her colleagues may hold about MLs, she must acknowledge her own positionality as a non-white educator and how that status affects her advocacy work. Advocating for MLs as an ML and person of color means that she may be perceived as being in conflict with her white, English-speaking colleagues. As her reflection illustrates, only by recognizing and navigating the power dynamics and politics at play in our own local contexts can we begin to account for the reality of what we may encounter as critical advocates.

Articulate Your Goal(s)

To hold ourselves and each other accountable, it is essential that we are transparent about what we hope to achieve through our critical advocacy action. Through goal-setting, critical advocates can articulate what changes they hope to make. Because engaging in critical advocacy is an interactive and dynamic process, we encourage you to think of your goal not as a fixed "endpoint" but as a living guidepost that evolves as you deepen your understanding of the issue. With that in mind, we encourage you to think about the following questions as you set your goal(s):

- Have I listened to and sought insight from others?
- Have I shifted based on others' feedback?
- How will I know if I've made progress or found success?

Approaching goal setting in this way, grounded in both structure and flexibility, encourages humility, reflection, and sustained commitment. There may be instances in which discrete, measurable goals may be helpful, particularly if you want to track progress and hold yourself and others accountable. Advocates interested in this approach might consider developing goals that are Specific, Measurable, Attainable, Relevant, and Time-Bound (SMART). Michelle, for example, developed the following goal and anticipated outcome to address the school-wide communication issues she identified:

Voices From the Field

By the end of the first semester, I will have a system of reminders set up to be distributed monthly to each [school] site via email, briefly outlining our translation and interpretation request process, given input from site leaders and stakeholders. When the reminders are sent, I expect to see utilization rates of our translation/interpretation tools and request forms increase from last year's/month's/semester's numbers. With increased communication, [I expect] feedback [from parents] regarding inclusion and understanding [of their] child's school system to also increase.

As you develop clear goals, you could revisit several *Digging In* activities that invited you to think about your critical advocacy actions. In Chapter 2, you redefined advocacy through a critical, asset-oriented lens, drawing attention to the ideologies that circulate through advocacy for MLs. In Chapter 4, you reflected on how you engage in advocacy action across the four branches and where you see room for growth. You can think about goal-setting around a "problem of practice" in your classroom or school and consider how you might do that effectively. And in Chapter 5, you reflected on a difficult critical advocacy experience that had a professional or interpersonal impact. You can consider what kind of goal you were pursuing in that instance, whose needs and perspectives were centered, and how you assessed what counted as "progress" toward meeting that goal.

Assess the Degree to Which You Achieved Your Goal(s)

Without a realistic and honest accounting of how our actions played out, critical advocates cannot improve, change course, or evolve their efforts. For this reason, the last stage of critical advocacy action planning involves being realistic about your own actions and your role in the process. We have developed the following questions that you can ask yourself throughout your critical advocacy actions. Some are helpful as continuous check-ins to ensure that your actions are proceeding meaningfully and effectively, and others are useful for reflecting on your actions after you have reached a goal (or not):

- What have I learned about this issue and about myself through this work?
- Did I achieve my goals? What helped me achieve them?
- Do my goals still reflect the voices and priorities of those with/for whom I am advocating?
- If I feel I did not achieve my goals, what kept me from finding success? How will I shift my approach as a result?
- How will I "fortify myself for the on-going struggle" (Kaba, 2025) that accompanies critical advocacy?

You'll notice that these questions also align with our core critical advocacy beliefs, the trunk of our tree. They reflect the importance of empathy and compassion for *ourselves* as we engage in critical advocacy work. These questions enable you to take stock of the work you are doing and what you are learning about both the issue and yourself so that you can continually expand and evolve your efforts. They emphasize the importance of collaboration and relationships. Continually checking in about whether our goals reflect the voices and priorities of MLs is integral to advocacy that rejects deficit-oriented, savioristic approaches. Finally, these questions drive you to be a perpetual learner. Acknowledging that critical advocacy action is a learning experience helps ensure that our efforts are sustainable. Being single-minded about a goal or a cause without continually assessing whether that goal or cause is still relevant or whether our actions are effective is lacking in self-awareness and flexibility, key elements of critical advocacy.

The questions included in this stage of the Critical Advocacy Action Planning Tool should ideally help you and those you are working with to stay grounded, self-aware, honest, and open to change. As you reflect throughout your work, you will also think about how you will fortify yourselves for the on-going struggle

(Kaba, 2025). Doing so requires not only a flexible, responsive plan, but a strong community, one that will both hold you accountable and sustain you so that you can continue to do good, meaningful work for MLs. You can revisit some of the ways we suggest sustaining your work through care of self and community in Chapter 5.

Conclusion

This chapter walked you through the Critical Advocacy Action Planning Tool. At each stage of the planning process, we included questions that you and those you engage in advocacy with can ask yourselves, ensuring that your plans are informed and go beyond good intentions. We also included excerpts from Michelle and Dr. Dilini's action plans to demonstrate the kind of thinking this process calls for. This planning will likely not play out in the linear way we have presented it. However, we hope it gives you a framework to organize your thoughts, plan for action, and check in with yourself and others throughout the process.

As you embark on critical advocacy action planning in your own local context, we hope you'll keep the metaphor of the tree in your mind. Critical advocacy action does not sprout on its own; those branches, off-shoots, and leaves grow when they are rooted in awareness of our identities and on-going experiences and supported by a firm, sturdy trunk of core, asset-oriented beliefs. When we think of critical advocacy as this kind of holistic system, our actions are more likely to be meaningful, sustainable, and effective for MLs, for your community, and for *you* as a critical advocate.

Conclusion

Planting Seeds for the Critical Advocacy Work Ahead

To be a critical advocate for MLs means walking a line. On one side of the line, critical advocates must be aware of the stark realities faced by MLs, their families, and their communities. As we finish writing this book, we see news alerts of daycare workers taken in broad daylight by masked ICE agents outside their places of work. We hear disparaging, racist rants about Somali immigrants by the President of the United States and his administration. We see the decimation of the Department of Education and the federal funding for MLs held hostage. We see the on-going exodus from the field of teaching and resulting teacher shortages that leave MLs underserved and overburden the educators who stay. Being aware of and responsive to these realities is integral to critical advocacy for MLs.

On the other side of the line, critical advocates must maintain hope if they are to continue their work on behalf of MLs in schools. We must recognize the power of people on the ground to shape their local realities. Alongside the troubling and disillusioning stories we see on the news and across our social media feeds, we also see communities hosting Know Your Rights trainings and raising awareness about how to defend immigrant

DOI: 10.4324/9781003628774-12

neighbors. We see people donating to community refrigerators and local food banks so that those who are afraid to leave their homes do not go hungry. And more than anything, we see our fellow educators show up to schools every single day to serve their ML students with care and compassion.

To walk this line, critical advocates must enter advocacy work with eyes wide open, aware of the barriers, challenges, and repercussions that may result from their efforts. The truth is that critical advocates cannot know what lies ahead, but we can prepare ourselves by deepening and extending our roots, strengthening our trunks, and growing healthy branches that sprout leaves of meaningful local advocacy action. Part of that preparation includes recognizing that this socio-political season is not the first, nor will it be the last, in which MLs are under attack. Though we are in a moment of crisis, we remind you that critical advocacy is not solely reactive. For critical advocacy to be sustainable, it must be ongoing and enacted over time, not just during a crisis. For this reason, this book has focused less on the *what* (i.e., the specific topics and issues facing MLs that require advocacy) and more on the *how* (i.e., how we develop the stance and practices that enable us to engage in *any* advocacy efforts ethically and critically). We believe that part of the "how" of critical advocacy is learning to live and work on both sides of that line, with eyes wide open about ourselves and our work, the historical contexts in which we advocate, and our short- and long-term vision for educating MLs.

With this in mind, we conclude the book by planting a few "seeds" for the critical advocacy work that lies ahead. These seeds come from our Voices from the Field interviews with critical advocates whose work has spanned many seasons. What these educators have learned, and how their work has evolved and changed across seasons of their lives and careers, has equipped them with the humility and wisdom to engage in critical advocacy over time. Their words help us recognize that advocacy work is personal, shaped by who we are, political, shaped by larger systems and structures, and pedagogical, deeply embedded in everything we do with and for ML students in schools. Their voices and insights have reminded us of the importance of approaching critical advocacy for MLs with both honesty and hope, and we hope they do the same for you.

Seed #1: Our Roots and Trunk Can Sustain Us Through Different Seasons of Critical Advocacy Action

As we have said throughout the book, meaningful, sustainable, and effective critical advocacy is deeply tied to who we are and what we believe. The roots that we forge in our early years are a part of that identity and belief system, as are the roots that continue to grow with our on-going personal and professional experiences. Those roots support a sturdy trunk, which is made up of what we described in Chapter 3 as core beliefs in the power of empathy and compassion, collaboration and relationships, and perpetual learning. From that well-supported trunk grow branches and leaves of local action that lead to positive change for MLs. Those leaves of local action can and *must* grow differently across different times and contexts, for different audiences, and in response to different opportunities and constraints. On this, Katie and Michelle offer important insights:

Voices From the Field

> I have like five more years until I'm at 30 years of teaching, so I'll be eligible for retirement at that point. I think after that, I'm going down to the border to learn more about what's going on there. This is my life's calling. I really like photography. I thought about trying to document some things that are going on in different places, just to have photographs and stories of people, to make it more accessible. This is a human, and this is their story.
>
> – Katie, English as a Second Language teacher, Colorado

> The systems here are really broken. They were always broken, but [COVID-19] shined a spotlight on it for me. My eyes were opened. So then I made this commitment to myself. I was like, I'm gonna fix the systems, which is a huge, pie-in-the-sky type of goal. I'm a visionary. I'm a dreamer. And that's when I started thinking about what type of role I needed to advocate for, and I advocated for it in a different district. And so that's when I shifted into this role [of district-level coordinator].
>
> – Michelle, Multilingual Family Engagement Specialist and English Learner Instructional Coach, Wisconsin

Critical advocates' roots and trunk sustain them through seasons of change in their lives and careers and nourish their future growth. For Katie, her passion for working with MLs – which she refers to as her "life's calling" – extends beyond the classroom. Though she is close to retirement, she is already envisioning the next directions in which her branches may grow. In turning from ESL teaching to photography, from the classroom to the US-Mexico border, we see how Katie's core belief in the humanity of her ML students and of immigrants in general will sustain and evolve her actions in the next season of her critical advocacy work.

For Michelle, the difficult season of the COVID-19 pandemic "shined a spotlight" on just how "broken" the systems of support for MLs are. Rather than completely discouraging her, this awareness helped her envision *better* systems and to dream beyond the inequities of the moment. With eyes wide open about what the MLs in her community truly needed, Michelle envisioned a new role, moving from being a classroom teacher to a district coordinator of services for MLs, where she could make even more impact. In this way, her roots and trunk, strong in the belief that MLs deserve an equitable education, helped her both acknowledge difficult realities *and* imagine a future for herself and her ML students that did not yet exist.

Seed #2: Critical Advocacy Requires Deep and Outward Growth to Be Sustainable

Critical advocacy must be sustainable, and we believe that sustainability is strengthened through advocates' own critical self-awareness as well as their relationships with others. Conversely, unsustainable approaches to advocacy are often rooted in biased and unbounded individualism; one lone advocate forging ahead no matter the warnings they are given, the bridges they burn, or the parts of themselves they give up in the process. Such an approach is often ineffective as it does not attend to the creation of systems and relationships that ensure that the advocacy is on-going rather than dependent on individuals. Nicole and Jenny spoke about these ideas:

Voices From the Field

> I want to train teachers one day. I want to be an adjunct [professor] or something. I want to teach teachers going into it – like, how can you help, what are ways that you can help these students?
>
> – Nicole, English as a Second Language teacher, New Jersey

> Most advocates struggle with helping other people advocate because we're used to fixing it, right? Like I'm used to fixing the problem because I have a lot of experience, so I can tell you how to fix it. But as I saw in one of my last environments, when I stepped out, everything fell apart because there was no sustainability. And so people would reach out and go, "Hey, how do we do this? How do we do that?" That is something we all struggle with, but me especially, how can I teach you how to do it instead of me trying to handle it all by myself?
>
> – Jenny, English Language Instructional Specialist, Oklahoma

Nicole and Jenny explore what it means to imagine influence and impact beyond themselves. Rather than center their own individual critical advocacy actions, they emphasize the importance of sustainability through deep and outward growth. When we picture sustainability through the tree metaphor, we envision an ever-deepening and spreading root structure, a trunk that grows not only tall but wide, with roots that are nourished by the roots of others and branches and leaves that extend further and further outward. Nicole and Jenny speak to the power of investing in others and thus broadening their critical advocacy efforts. Nicole envisions a future in teacher education, helping young teachers of MLs to see where and how they can help. Jenny's desire for sustainability emerges from being honest about *herself*; she is aware of her own tendency to go in and "fix it," rather than collaborate and teach others. Though Jenny is still grappling with these ideas, she and Nicole are forging deeper understandings of themselves and broadening their relationships with others in order to engage in critical advocacy efforts that are more sustainable and far-reaching.

Seed #3: We Must Move "From Fighting to Hoping" in Critical Advocacy Work

In our conversations with critical advocates, many told stories of changes in mindset toward their advocacy work. They spoke about how they had matured and evolved, moving from, as Jenny put it in Chapter 5, being a "wrecking ball," taking down any barrier in their path, to approaching advocacy through thoughtful strategizing, relationships, and care.

Voices From the Field

I think it comes with age, recognizing that being the loudest person in the room isn't always how you get your message across. I'm feisty, and I'd say that for a long time, advocacy was equivalent to fighting.

> Over the years, growing with age and experience, I've realized that most people want to do the right thing for kids. [I have to] assume positive intent. So I try to do that and help address misconceptions. This is a teaching experience. If [someone] is coming to me with a question, it's because they care, because they want to do the right thing. They want to help. And that's what I'm here for. So I would say over time, I've shifted from this idea that I'm fighting something to I'm hoping.
>
> – Grace, Director of World Languages and English as a New Language, New York

Grace speaks to a shift in mindset and approach, describing how her understanding of advocacy has evolved from being "equivalent to fighting" to both "teaching" and "hoping." We want to distinguish here between fighting as a metaphor for seeking justice in inequitable systems and fighting as being "the loudest person in the room" who impulsively takes on anything and anyone as they engage in advocacy. Fighting as a metaphor is incredibly important; we must have "fight" in us – resilience, inner strength, courage – if we are to take on injustices and work with marginalized communities. Literal fighting, as Grace has come to realize, "isn't always how you get your message across."

Grace's current approach to messaging takes the form of assuming people's positive intent and addressing misconceptions as they arise. In short, she sees critical advocacy work as *teaching*. Teaching, just like critical advocacy, is an act of hope, in that we may never know exactly how it takes root. Grace cannot know how her commitment to addressing misconceptions – asking questions, pushing thinking, providing alternative interpretations, offering new approaches – will impact her colleagues' journeys. In teaching others, Grace is cultivating an interconnected root system that sustains both individual educators' trees and the community, or forest, as a whole.

Grace's seed of wisdom is one we take with us into our own work. In writing this book, we have tried to do exactly what we've asked you to do: explore our own roots with self-awareness and criticality, define the core beliefs that strengthen our trunks, and extend the branches that help us enact what we believe. This book is one such branch, and we hope that from it will sprout leaves of local action – our own and *yours* – that support MLs in schools. We approach this work with eyes wide open; we know the ideological and structural barriers that stand in the way of educational equity for MLs, and that struggle will always accompany advocacy action. But like Grace, and like so many of you, we choose *teaching* and we choose *hope* as we take on the critical advocacy work that lies ahead. We close, as we began, with the words of Dr. Ernest Morrell:

> Think of the struggle as beautiful because you are embracing it. You are embracing a legacy of people who have struggled on behalf of what is right. Unfortunately, in this world we live in, working for what is right will always be a struggle. . . . Critical hope is essential to our future as a profession as it has been essential to our past. The next movement will be fueled by it.
>
> (2015, p. 326)

As Dr. Morrell reminds us, when we engage in struggle, we become part of a living legacy. We hope this book has provided you with both hope and tools you can use as you forge more just futures for MLs.

References

Accurso, K., Lopez Rodriguez, S., & Lopez, A. (2019). Challenging deficit perspectives of multilingual learners in everyday talk. *Currents, 42*(1), 39–41. https://www.researchgate.net/profile/Kathryn-Accurso/publication/335603248_Challenging_Deficit_Perspectives_of_Multilingual_Learners_in_Everyday_Talk/links/5d6fa08f4585151ee49b9199/Challenging-Deficit-Perspectives-of-Multilingual-Learners-in-Everyday-Talk.pdf

Arias, M.B., & Morillo-Campbell, M. (2008). Promoting ELL parental involvement: Challenges in contested times. *Education Public Interest Center*. http://files.eric.ed.gov/fulltext/ED506652.pdf

Ascenzi-Moreno, L. (2018). Translanguaging and responsive assessment adaptations: Emergent bilingual readers through the lens of possibility. *Language Arts, 95*(6), 355–369. https://doi.org/10.58680/la201829683

Athanases, S.Z., & De Oliveira, L.C. (2008). Advocacy for equity in classrooms and beyond: New teachers' challenges and responses. *Teachers College Record, 110*(1), 64–104. https://doi.org/10.1177/016146810811000101

Bakhtin, M.M. (1981). *The Dialogic imagination: Four essays* (M. Holquist, Ed.; C. Emerson & M. Holquist, Trans.). University of Texas Press.

Baum, S.E. (2023, May 16). Kelly Hayes and Mariame Kaba on their new handbook for radical organizing. *The Nation*. https://www.thenation.com/article/activism/kelly-hayes-mariame-kaba-radicalize-you/

Brasof, M. (2015). *Student voice and school governance: Distributing leadership to youth and adults*. Routledge.

Campano, G., Ghiso, M.P., & Welch, B.J. (2016). *Partnering with immigrant communities: Action through literacy*. Teachers College Press. https://doi.org/10.1080/15595692.2016.1277698

Chen, C.W., & Gorski, P.C. (2015). Burnout in social justice and human rights activists: Symptoms, causes and implications. *Journal of Human Rights Practice, 7*(3), 366–390. https://doi.org/10.1093/jhuman/huv011

Cheruvu, R., Souto-Manning, M., Lencl, T., & Chin-Calubaquib, M. (2015). Race, isolation, and exclusion: What early childhood teacher educators need to know about the experiences of pre-service teachers of color. *The Urban Review*, *47*(2), 237–265. https://doi.org/10.1007/s11256-014-0291-8

Cooper, C.R., Chavira, G., & Mena, D.D. (2005). From pipelines to partnerships: A synthesis of research on how diverse families, schools, and communities support children's pathways through school. *Journal of Education for Students Placed at Risk*, *10*(4), 407–430. https://doi.org/10.1207/s15327671espr1004_4

Crenshaw, K. (1989). Demarginalizing the intersection of race and sex: A Black feminist critique of antidiscrimination doctrine, feminist theory and antiracist politics. *The University of Chicago Legal Forum*, *1989*, 139. https://scholarship.law.columbia.edu/faculty_scholarship/3007

Crenshaw, K. (1991). Mapping the margins: Intersectionality, identity politics, and violence against women of color. *Stanford Law Review*, *43*(6), 1241–1299. https://doi.org/10.2307/1229039

Cuban, L. (2025, March 13). Teachers are street-level bureaucrats who make classroom policies. *Larry Cuban on School Reform and Classroom Practice*. https://larrycuban.wordpress.com/2025/03/13/teachers-are-street-level-bureaucrats-who-make-classroom-policies/

Dabach, D.B. (2014). "I am not a shelter!": Stigma and social boundaries in teachers' accounts of students' experience in separate "sheltered" English learner classrooms. *Journal of Education for Students Placed at Risk (JESPAR)*, *19*(2), 98–124. https://doi-org.ezproxy.rowan.edu/10.1080/10824669.2014.954044

de Jong, E.J., & Harper, C.A. (2005). Preparing mainstream teachers for English-language learners: Is being a good teacher good enough? *Teacher Education Quarterly*, *32*(2), 101–124.

Delgado, R. (1989). Storytelling for oppositionists and others: A plea for narrative. *Michigan Law Review*, *87*(8), 2411–2441. https://doi.org/10.2307/1289308

de Sousa Santos, B. (2018). *The end of the cognitive empire: The coming of age of epistemologies of the South*. Duke University Press.

Dove, M.G., & Honigsfeld, A. (2017). *Co-teaching for English learners: A guide to collaborative planning, instruction, assessment, and reflection*. Corwin Press.

Dubetz, N.E., & de Jong, E.J. (2011). Teacher advocacy in bilingual programs. *Bilingual Research Journal*, *34*(3), 248–262. https://doi.org/10.1080/15235882.2011.623603

Duncan, K.E. (2020). "That's my job": Black teachers' perspectives on helping Black students navigate white supremacy. *Race Ethnicity and Education*, *25*(7), 978–996. https://doi.org/10.1080/13613324.2020.17377

Ebarvia, T. (2019). Keynote address. Presentation, International Literacy Association, New Orleans, LA, October 12.

The Education Trust. (2018). Our stories, our struggles, our strengths: Perspectives and reflections from Latino teachers. https://www.educationevolving.org/files/Our-Stories-Our-Struggles-Our-Strengths-FINAL.pdf

Evans, K., Oliveira, G., Hason III, R.G., Crea, T.M., Neville, S.E., & Fitchett, V. (2022). Unaccompanied children's education in the United States: Service provider's perspective on challenges and support strategies. *Cultura Educación Sociedad*, *13*(1), 193–218.

Every Student Succeeds Act, 20 U.S.C. § 6301. (2015). https://www.congress.gov/114/plaws/publ95/PLAW-114publ95.pdf

Flores, N. (2015, July 6). What if we talked about monolingual White children the way we talk about low-income children of color? https://educationallinguist.wordpress.com/2015/07/06/what-if-we-talked-about-monolingual-white-children-the-way-we-talk-about-low-income-children-of-color/

Flores, N., & Rosa, J. (2015). Undoing appropriateness: Raciolinguistic ideologies and language diversity in education. *Harvard Educational Review*, *85*(2), 149–171. https://doi.org/10.17763/0017-8055.85.2.149

Freire, P. (1970). *Pedagogy of the oppressed*. Continuum.

García, O. (2009). *Bilingualism in the 21st century: A global perspective*. Wiley-Blackwell.

García, O., Flores, N., Seltzer, K., Wei, L., Otheguy, R., & Rosa, J. (2021). Rejecting abyssal thinking in the language and education of racialized bilinguals: A manifesto. *Critical Inquiry in Language Studies*, *18*(3), 203–228. https://doi.org/10.1080/15427587.2021.1935957

García, O., & Kleifgen, J. (2018). *Educating emergent bilinguals: Policies, programs, and practices for English learners* (2nd ed.). Teachers College Press.

García, O., Seltzer, K., & Witt, D. (2018). Disrupting linguistic inequalities in US urban classrooms: The role of translanguaging. In P. Van Avermaet, S. Slembrouck, K. Van Gorp, S. Sierens, & K. Maryns (Eds.), *The multilingual edge of education* (pp. 41–66). Palgrave Macmillan. https://doi.org/10.1057/978-1-137-54856-6_3

García, O., & Torres-Guevara, R. (2009). *Monoglossic ideologies and language policies in the education of U.S. Latinas/os*. Routledge.

Ghast, M.J., Chisholm, J.S., & Sivira-Gonzalez, Y. (2022). Racialization of 'ESL students' in a diverse school and multilingual Latina/o peer mentors. *Race Ethnicity and Education*, *27*(7), 1010–1030. https://doi.org/10.1080/13613324.2022.2069737

Gibbons, P. (2014). *Scaffolding language, scaffolding learning: Teaching English language learners in the mainstream classroom* (2nd ed.). Heinemann.

González, N., Moll, L.C., & Amanti, C. (2005). *Funds of knowledge: Theorizing practices in households, communities, and classrooms*. Routledge.

Gorski, P.C., & Erakat, N. (2019). Racism, whiteness, and burnout in antiracism movements: How white racial justice activists elevate burnout in racial justice activists of color in the United States. *Ethnicities*, *19*(5), 784–808. https://doi.org/10.1177/1468796819833871

Hammond, Z. (2014). *Culturally responsive teaching and the brain: Promoting authentic engagement and rigor among culturally and linguistically diverse students*. Corwin.

Hattie, J. (2016). Third Annual Visible Learning Conference: Mindframes and Maximizers, Washington, DC, July 11.

Hernández-Johnson, M., Taylor, V., Singh, R., Marrun, N.A., Plachowski, T.J., & Clark, C. (2023). "Like where are those teachers?": A critical race theory analysis of teachers of color who have "left" teaching. *International Journal of Qualitative Studies in Education*, *36*(10), 1924–1944. https://doi.org/10.1080/09518398.2021.1956634

hooks, b. (1994). *Teaching to transgress: Education as the practice of freedom*. Routledge.

Huang, Y., & Zhou, L. (2025). Self-care strategies for preservice teachers: A scoping review. *Teachers and Teaching*, 1–19. https://doi.org/10.1080/13540602.2025.2502952

Kaba, M. (2025). Making an activism/organizing plan: A template [zine]. *One Million Experiments, 8*, 1–25. https://millionexperiments.com/zines/making-a-plan

Kohli, R. (2018). Behind school doors: The impact of hostile racial climates on urban teachers of color. *Urban Education, 53*(3), 307–333.

Kohli, R., Picower, B., Martinez, A., & Ortiz, N. (2015). Critical professional development: Centering the social justice needs of teachers. *International Journal of Critical Pedagogy, 6*(2), 7–24.

Lee, S., Woo, A., Kaufman, J.H., & Doan, S. (2025). *Lost in translation–teachers report feeling unprepared to support multilingual learners*. RAND American Educator Panels. https://www.rand.org/content/dam/rand/pubs/research_reports/RRA100/RRA134-29/RAND_RRA134-29.pdf

Lippi-Green, R. (2012). *English with an accent: Language, ideology and discrimination in the United States* (2nd ed.). Routledge.

Love, B.L. (2019). *We want to do more than survive: Abolitionist teaching and the pursuit of educational freedom*. Beacon Press.

Maldonado Torres, S.E. (2022). Demystifying Latinos parental involvement in school activities. *Journal of Latinos and Education, 21*(4), 404–410. https://doi.org/10.1080/15348431.2019.1680375

Martínez-Roldán, C. (2013). The representation of Latinos and the use of Spanish: A critical content analysis of "Skippyjon Jones". *Journal of Children's Literature, 39*(1), 5–14.

Menken, K., & García, O. (2010). *Negotiating language policies in schools: Educators as policymakers*. Routledge.

Menken, K., & Sánchez, M.T. (2019). Translanguaging in English-only schools: From pedagogy to stance in the disruption of monolingual policies and practices. *TESOL: Quarterly, 53*(3), 741–767. https://doi.org/10.1002/tesq.513

Mentor, M., & Sealey-Ruiz, Y. (2021). Doing the deep work of antiracist pedagogy: Toward self-excavation for equitable classroom teaching. *Language Arts, 99*(1), 19–24. https://doi.org/10.58680/la202131410

Morrell, E. (2015). The 2014 NCTE presidential address: Powerful English at NCTE yesterday, today, and tomorrow: Toward the next movement. *Research in the Teaching of English, 49*(3), 307–327.

National Education Association. (2023, May 17). Power mapping 101. https://www.nea.org/professional-excellence/student-engagement/tools-tips/power-mapping-101

Noguera, P.A. (2009). *The trouble with black boys: . . . and other reflections on race, equity, and the future of public education*. John Wiley & Sons.

Palmer, D.K. (2018). Supporting bilingual teachers to be leaders for social change: "I must create advocates for biliteracy". *International Multilingual Research Journal*, *12*(3), 203–216. https://doi.org/10.1080/19313152.2018.1474063

Paris, D., & Alim, H.S. (Eds.). (2017). *Culturally sustaining pedagogies: Teaching and learning for justice in a changing world*. Teachers College Press.

Pereira, N., & de Oliveira, L.C. (2022). Multilingual learners with high academic potential. In J.L. Roberts, T.F. Inman, & J.H. Robins (Eds.), *Introduction to gifted education* (2nd ed., pp. 403–419). Routledge.

Picower, B. (2012). *Practice what you teach: Social justice education in the classroom and the streets*. Routledge.

Poza, L.E. (2021). Adding flesh to the bones: Dignity frames for English learner education. *Harvard Educational Review*, *91*(4), 482–510. https://doi.org/10.17763/1943-5045-91.4.482

Raymond, K.M., Ethridge, E.A., & Fields, K. (2025). What it takes to be an advocate: Teachers' perceptions of their strengths and challenges. *Action in Teacher Education*, *47*(1), 46–62. https://doi.org/10.1080/01626620.2024.2383744

Rodriguez, Y. (2024). Latina: Leading while silencing imposter syndrome. In A.H. Wang & M. Gorgan (Eds.), *Intersectionality and leading social change in education: Professional learning to transform self, others, and the field* (pp. 73–84). Routledge.

Samuels, S. (2021). Why they struggle to stay: Black women educators reflect on the state of teachers. *The Clearing House: A Journal of Educational Strategies, Issues, and Ideas*, *94*(3), 137–150. https://doi.org/10.1080/00098655.2021.1907145

Sánchez, M.T., García, O., & Solorza, C. (2018). Reframing language allocation policy in dual language bilingual education. *Bilingual Research Journal*, *41*(1), 37–51. https://doi.org/10.1080/15235882.2017.1405098

Sánchez, M.T., & Menken, K. (2020). Emergent bilingual leadership teams: Distributed leadership in CUNY-NYSIEB schools. In CUNY-NYSIEB (Ed.), *Translanguaging and transformative teaching for emergent bilingual students* (pp. 67–78). Routledge.

Schachner, J. (2005). *Skippyjon Jones*. Dutton Books for Young Readers.

Schissel, J.L. (2019). *Social consequences of testing for language-minoritized bilinguals in the United States* (Vol. 117). Multilingual Matters.

Sealey-Ruiz, Y. (2022). An archaeology of self for our times: Another talk to teachers. *English Journal, 111*(5), 21–26. https://doi.org/10.58680/ej202231819

Seltzer, K. (2022). Enacting a critical translingual approach in teacher preparation: Disrupting oppressive language ideologies and fostering the personal, political, and pedagogical stances of pre-service teachers of English. *TESOL Journal, 13*(2), e649. https://doi.org/10.1002/tesj.649

Seltzer, K., Johnson, S.I., & García, O. (2025). *The translanguaging classroom: Leveraging student bilingualism for learning* (2nd ed.). Brookes Publishing.

Serviss, J. (2022, May 13). 4 benefits of an active professional learning community. *International Society for Technology in Education.* https://iste.org/blog/4-benefits-of-an-active-professional-learning-community

Shelby-Caffey, C., Abril-Gonzalez, P., & Salazar Pérez, M. (2022). Excavating the methodological terrains of life writing: How and why we engage in re-memberings of Black and Chicana/Latina lived experiences. In L.E. Bailey & K. Hinton (Eds.), *Racial dimensions of life writing in education* (pp. 83–105). Information Age Publishing.

Shuck, G. (2009). Racializing the nonnative English speaker. *Journal of Language, Identity & Education*, *5*(4), 259–276. https://doi.org/10.1207/s15327701jlie0504_1

Solórzano, D.G., & Yosso, T.J. (2002). Critical race methodology: Counter-storytelling as an analytic framework or education research. *Qualitative Inquiry*, *8*(1), 23–44. https://doi.org/10.1177/107780040200800103

Song, K. (2023). Cherishing immigrant parents' aspiration to support multilingual children's literacy development across languages. *The Reading Teacher*, *77*(2), 238–242. https://doi-org.ezproxy.rowan.edu/10.1002/trtr.2231

Southern Poverty Law Center. (2012, November 27). Unlocking your community's hidden strengths: A guidebook to community asset-mapping. https://www.splcenter.org/resources/reports/unlocking-your-communitys-hidden-strengths-guidebook-community-asset-mapping/

Suarez, M., & Dominguez, M. (2015). "Carrying the weight": ESL teacher negotiations toward advocacy and equity. *Radical Pedagogy, 12*(2), 46–67.

Suh, S., & Michener, C.J. (2024). Collaborative advocacy for multilingual learners: Developments from coursework into practice. *TESOL Journal, 15*(4), 1–18. https://doi.org/10.1002%2Ftesj.827

Thorstensson Dávila, L. (2013). Learning English and "Smartness": Refugee students negotiate language, reception, and ability in school. *Journal of Southeast Asian American Education & Advancement, 8*(1), 1–19. https://www.jstor.org/stable/48684529

Valdés, G. (1996). *Con respeto: Bridging the distances between culturally diverse families and schools: An ethnographic portrait*. Teachers College Press.

Valdés, G. (2014). The world outside and inside schools: Language and immigrant children. In M.M. Suárez-Orozco, C. Suárez-Orozco, & D. Qin-Hilliard (Eds.), *The new immigrant and language* (pp. 152–166). Routledge.

Valenzuela, A. (1999). *Subtractive schooling: US-Mexican youth and the politics of caring*. State University of New York Press.

Wang, Y., & Li, S. (2020). Issues, challenges, and future directions for multilingual assessment. *Journal of Language Teaching and Research, 11*(6), 914–919. http://dx.doi.org/10.17507/jltr.1106.06

Wright, W.E. (2025). *Foundations for teaching English language learners: Research, theory, policy, and practice* (4th ed.). Brookes Publishing.

Yosso, T.J. (2005). Whose culture has capital? A critical race theory discussion of community cultural wealth. *Race Ethnicity and Education, 8*(1), 69–91. https://doi.org/10.1080/1361332052000341006

Appendix A

Critical Advocacy Action Planning Tool

We have organized this tool around the five stages of critical advocacy action. For each stage, we have adapted the guiding questions to streamline your planning and reflection. We also include "Digging In" features from the book that are relevant to each stage. We encourage you to revisit the Critical Advocacy Action Planning Connections at the end of each chapter to ground your planning. You can access a downloadable version of this tool at Routledge.com/9781041045526.

<table>
<tr><td colspan="2">1. Identify an issue, opportunity, or area of concern that relates to MLs in your context</td></tr>
<tr><td>Planning & Reflection</td><td>♦ How are aspects of my roots shaping my interpretations and efforts?
♦ Why does this issue matter to me?
♦ How did I come to learn about this issue? Who raised it?
♦ What assumptions am I making about this issue?</td></tr>
<tr><td>Support</td><td>Introduction
♦ Digging in: Defining Your Advocacy
Chapter 1
♦ Digging In: Exploring Your Roots
Chapter 2
♦ Digging In: Exploring Deficit-Oriented Ideologies and Policies
♦ Digging In: (Re)defining Advocacy Through a Critical, Asset-Oriented Lens</td></tr>
<tr><td colspan="2">2. Brainstorm how you can address this issue, opportunity, or concern.</td></tr>
<tr><td>Planning & Reflection</td><td>♦ What action(s) can I take to address this issue?
♦ What collaborations and learning opportunities will help me address this issue?
♦ What are my strengths, and how can I use them in my advocacy?
♦ How am I incorporating the needs/perspectives of those I am trying to advocate for into this goal?</td></tr>
<tr><td>Support</td><td>Chapter 3
♦ Digging In: Resources for Community Building
Chapter 4
♦ Digging In (see all 4 of the 4 Branches of Critical Advocacy Action)</td></tr>
</table>

3. Think through this issue in terms of your local context.	
Planning & Reflection	♦ What are local perspectives of MLs? How will I account for these perspectives? ♦ Is the way I want to address this issue actually viable and safe in my context? ♦ Have I learned enough about who is already doing this work/what resources already exist? ♦ What consequences might I face in carrying out this action? How will I contend with them?
Support	Chapter 2 ♦ Digging In: Adopting a Critical Asset-Oriented Lens Chapter 4 ♦ Digging In: Relationship-Building and Community Connections as Critical Advocacy ♦ Digging In: Disrupting Deficit-Oriented Thinking about MLs Chapter 5 ♦ Digging In: Exploring the Challenges of Critical Advocacy ♦ Digging In: Knowing the Interpersonal Dynamics of your Context Chapter 6 ♦ Digging In (see all 4 of the 4 scenarios of critical advocacy in action)
4. Articulate your goal.	
Planning & Reflection	♦ In developing my goal(s), have I sought insights from others, listened to others enough and/or shifted based on others' feedback? ♦ How will I know if I've made progress/found success?
Support	Chapter 2 ♦ Digging In: Adopting a Critical Asset-Oriented Lens Chapter 4 ♦ Digging In: Relationship-Building and Community Connections as Critical Advocacy ♦ Digging In: Pedagogical Decision-Making as Critical Advocacy ♦ Digging In: Local Policy-Making as Critical Advocacy Chapter 5 ♦ Digging In: Exploring Challenges of Critical Advocacy Chapter 6 ♦ Digging In (see all 4 of the 4 scenarios of critical advocacy in action)
5. Assess the degree to which you achieved your goal(s).	
Planning & Reflection	♦ Did I achieve my goal(s)? What helped me achieve it? ♦ If I did not achieve my goal(s), what kept me from finding success? How will I shift my approach as a result? ♦ Do my goals still reflect the voices and priorities of those with whom I am advocating? ♦ What have I learned about this issue and about myself? ♦ How will I "fortify myself for the on-going struggle" (Kaba, 2025) that accompanies critical advocacy?
Support	Chapter 5 ♦ Digging In: Exploring the Challenges of Critical Advocacy Chapter 6 ♦ Digging In (see all 4 of the 4 scenarios of critical advocacy in action)

For Product Safety Concerns and Information please contact our EU representative GPSR@taylorandfrancis.com
Taylor & Francis Verlag GmbH, Kaufingerstraße 24, 80331 München, Germany

www.ingramcontent.com/pod-product-compliance
Lightning Source LLC
LaVergne TN
LVHW010838120826
845149LV00017B/3274

* 9 7 8 1 0 4 1 0 4 5 5 2 6 *